9 - 75

The Myth of the
Independent Voter

The Myth of the Independent Voter

Bruce E. Keith, David B. Magleby,
Candice J. Nelson, Elizabeth Orr,
Mark C. Westlye, and
Raymond E. Wolfinger

UNIVERSITY OF CALIFORNIA PRESS
BERKELEY LOS ANGELES OXFORD

University of California Press
Berkeley and Los Angeles, California

University of California Press, Ltd.
Oxford, England

© 1992 by
The Regents of the University of California

Library of Congress Cataloging-in-Publication Data

The myth of the independent voter / Bruce E. Keith . . . [et al.].
  p. cm.
Includes bibliographical references and index.
ISBN 0-520-03688-3 (cloth).—ISBN 0-520-07720-2 (paper)
  1. Party affiliation—United States. 2. Political parties—United
States. 3. Voting—United States. 4. United States—Politics and
government—1945–   I. Keith, Bruce E.
JK2261.M97 1992
324.973—dc20   91-3636
                                                                           CIP

Printed in the United States of America
1 2 3 4 5 6 7 8 9

The paper used in this publication meets the minimum requirements of
American National Standard for Information Sciences—Permanence of
Paper for Printed Library Materials, ANSI Z39.48-1984.♾

*To the University of California
at Berkeley*

Contents

Figures

Tables

Preface

Thirty-five years ago a cartoon by Bill Maudlin had a man explaining his outlook on politics. "Me, I vote the man, not the party. Hoover, Landon, Dewey, Eisenhower. . . ." Most Americans resemble that man: they claim to vote for the best candidate, but their choices have a certain uniformity. Such predictable voting patterns reflect durable individual attachments to a party. Although these inclinations have long been recognized, their measurement has been possible only since the advent of survey research. A Democrat or Republican is someone who picks that identity when given a chance to do so by an interviewer. Almost all others call themselves Independents.

Most Americans who tell an interviewer that they are Independents will, if asked, concede that they are closer to the Democratic or Republican party. What should be made of this additional piece of information? For decades most academic specialists evidently concluded that the correct answer was "Nothing." The concession of closeness to a party was widely ignored and everyone who claimed to be an Independent was left in that one category, assumed to consist of people who were without partisan feelings.

These apparently neutral citizens did not attract much attention when they amounted to little more than a fifth of the electorate. But it was quite a different matter when, beginning in the late 1960s, their share of the voting-age population almost doubled to the point where nearly two out of five Americans seemed uncommitted to either major party. This was judged an event of the profoundest importance, perhaps the most significant domestic political development since the Vietnam War.

This book results from our discovery in the fall of 1974 that the key to understanding Independents is the hitherto ignored second question about closeness to a party. Independents who say they are closer to a party are very similar to outright identifiers with that party. Genuine neutrals amount to little more than a third of all those who first claim to be Independents. Our finding contradicted two groups of scholars— those architects of the first national surveys whose published writings treated all Independents as similar and the later revisionists whose thesis that the public was adrift without familiar reference points depended on the assumption that all Independents were alike in their neutrality.

As might be expected of a project that spans three decades, we have been helped by many people. Our earliest ventures into data analysis were aided by Margaret Baker and Ilona Einowski of the University of California, Berkeley. Steven J. Rosenstone and John R. Zaller gave us sage advice at the outset, as did Henry E. Brady many years later. We are grateful to Steven Rosenstone and Edward R. Tufte for comments on earlier drafts of parts of this book, and to Warren E. Miller for advice in the final stages. Our greatest debt is to Laura Stoker, whose meticulous, wise, and learned comments on our manuscript went well beyond the call of collegiality.

We gratefully acknowledge the contributions of our talented research assistants, including Martin I. Gilens, James M. Glaser, Michael G. Hagen, Benjamin Highton, and Jonathan S. Krasno of the University of California at Berkeley and Debbie Owen Bell, Jamie Cook, Mark R. Devey, Harlan Hatfield, Earl Marshall, Robert C. Miller, George I. Monsivais, Kristin Sandberg, Rodney J. Symes, Kathleen E. Tait, and Erin A. Wilson at Brigham Young University. Preparation of the various drafts of the manuscript was accomplished with speed and good cheer by Lyn Lake at the University of California and Lani Gurr and Lisa Miller at Brigham Young University.

We appreciate the patient professionalism displayed by Valeurie Friedman, Amy Klatzkin, and Naomi Schneider of the University of California Press.

Financial support was provided by the College of Family, Home, and Social Sciences, the Department of Political Science, and the Young Scholar Award program, all at Brigham Young University.

This book is based on data from surveys by the Institute of Social Research of the University of Michigan, conducted since 1978 by Warren E. Miller and the National Election Studies, supported by long-term grants from the National Science Foundation. The data were made available by the Interuniversity Consortium for Political and Social Research through UC DATA (Data Archive and Technical Assistance) of the University of California and the Social Science Data Archive of Brigham Young University. Neither the collector of the data nor the Consortium is responsible for our analyses or interpretations.

1

Partisanship and Independence

Few contemporary domestic political themes have attracted more attention than the growing number of Americans who choose to call themselves Independents rather than Democrats or Republicans. As one textbook observed, "None of the other trends . . . can match the decline in partisanship and party vitality with respect to the sheer number of words written."[1] The decline of partisanship has been a rare point of consensus among commentators in all parts of the political arena. Scholars and journalists, liberals and conservatives, Democrats and Republicans—all agree on this point. The conservative publicist Kevin Phillips wrote in 1982 that "the most enduring phenomenon of the years since the war in Vietnam and Watergate has been the rise in the ranks of independents."[2] The authors of *The Changing American Voter*, judged the most distinguished contribution to political science in 1976, concluded that the "most dramatic political change in the American public over the past two decades has been the

1. David B. Hill and Norman R. Luttbeg, *Trends in American Electoral Behavior*, 2d ed. (Itasca, Ill.: F. E. Peacock, 1983), 32.
2. Kevin P. Phillips, *Post-Conservative America* (New York: Random House, 1982), 227.

decline of partisanship."[3] This view was shared a dozen years later by the *New York Times* reporter Hedrick Smith, who wrote that "the most important phenomenon of American politics in the past quarter century has been the rise of independent voters who have at times outnumbered Republicans."[4]

As we will see, not everyone shares this view. However, it remains the preferred interpretation of at least some specialists in voting behavior and a great many students of political parties. The decline of the parties is a favorite theme in American government textbooks, the repository of our discipline's conventional wisdom and the main source of undergraduates' understanding of the political system. Most writers outside political science—historians, authors of big-picture interpretations of the United States, journalists—seem to take for granted the proposition that many fewer American voters are now affected by party ties.

The implications attributed to this putative growth in independence are numerous and momentous. Independents are unconstrained by partisanship from responding to election-year appeals. If more and more voters are becoming Independents, there could be wider and wider swings between the parties. Presumably this is what leads some observers to write that the increase in the number of Independents portends greater political instability. Other anticipated consequences include weaker presidential mandates, richer opportunities for third parties, partisan realignment, a more fragmented Congress, and the end of the current party system. We will examine these predictions in more detail shortly.

The implications for social science are scarcely less important. Party identification is the "foundation" of the "edifice" of conceptualizing and measuring voting associated with the National Election Studies (NES) conducted since 1952 by the

3. Norman H. Nie, Sidney Verba, and John R. Petrocik, *The Changing American Voter*, enlarged ed. (Cambridge: Harvard University Press, 1979), 47.

4. Hedrick Smith, *The Power Game: How Washington Works* (New York: Random House, 1988), 671.

University of Michigan's Center for Political Studies.[5] For a generation, political scientists had believed that party identification powerfully affected voting decisions and perceptions of political events; it was "the central thread connecting the citizen and the political process."[6] Assumed to be a point of stability in individual behavior, party identification was the baseline against which researchers measured the impact of short-term forces like issues, candidates, and assessments of governmental performance.[7]

In its modern meaning, "party identification" is a product of survey research. Democrats, Republicans, and Independents are identified by asking respondents to put themselves in one of these three categories. The portentous trend from partisanship to independence reflects an increase in the proportion of respondents who tell interviewers that they consider themselves not Republicans or Democrats but Independents. In the Michigan NES, the share of Independents went from 19 to 23 percent in the 1952–1964 period to a high of 37

5. Donald R. Kinder and David O. Sears, "Public Opinion and Political Action," in *Handbook of Social Psychology*, vol. 2, 3d ed., ed. Gardner Lindzey and Elliot Aronson (New York: Random House, 1985), 684.

The Michigan election research has had various labels since 1952. In the early years it was identified with the university's Survey Research Center and then took the name of the Center for Political Studies (CPS) when that unit was formed in the 1960s. Although still conducted by the CPS, the research has been called the National Election Studies (NES) since the creation in 1977 of a national board of overseers consequent to the first long-term multimillion-dollar grant to the CPS from the National Science Foundation.

The Michigan Survey Research Center conducted a national sample survey of sorts in 1948. For a variety of reasons, this study has had little visibility or influence, so our chronology of "the Michigan school" begins with the 1952 study.

6. Nie, Verba, and Petrocik, *The Changing American Voter*, 73.

7. One well-known example is the central place of party identification in calculating the "normal vote," a method used to identify groups that respond in different ways in a given election. See Philip E. Converse, "The Concept of a Normal Vote," in Angus Campbell et al., *Elections and the Political Order* (New York: John Wiley and Sons, 1966), 9–39.

percent in 1978. In 1990, 36 percent of the NES sample called themselves Independents.]

Any NES respondent who claimed to be an Independent has always been asked if he or she was closer to one or the other party. Until we began our research, analysts of the NES data—the major source of information about individual political behavior—seldom paid attention to this follow-up question. Independents were all those people who claimed this status when answering the initial question about party identification. This book results from our discovery more than fifteen years ago that the second question is essential to an understanding of Independents because it enables analysts to distinguish genuine Independents from those who initially claim this status but then concede that they lean toward the Democrats or Republicans. [Thus we can dispel the assumption, once almost universal and still widespread, that all Independents—"the second largest group in the electorate"—share some characteristics that differentiate them in important ways from Republicans and Democrats.[8] *This assumption is wrong. Independents, defined inclusively, have little in common. They are more diverse than either Republicans or Democrats. Most of them are not uncommitted, and they are not a bloc. They are largely closet Democrats and Republicans.]*

Therefore, none of the large generalizations about Independents is correct because as Independents are usually defined, the category includes not one but three kinds of people. Most of the increase in Independents has occurred among the hidden partisans; the high-level speculations apply only to genuine Independents, whose increase has been rather modest.

The gist of our findings about Independents began to circulate among some political scientists as early as the summer of 1975 and was reported at the end of that year in a textbook

8. Gerald M. Pomper et al., *The Election of 1976* (New York: David McKay, 1977), 73. This estimate is more modest than that of Nie, Verba, and Petrocik, who call Independents "the largest group in the society" (*The Changing American Voter*, 346).

coauthored by one of us.[9] Our first full statement was in a paper delivered in the summer of 1977.[10] Many of our early findings could have been found one place or another in the literature. Some were mentioned as an aside, an unremarked table, or a paragraph ignored in subsequent chapters. Despite some published clues and an unimaginable number of similar findings in computer printouts, our case against the monolithic conception of Independents was very much a minority view in 1977. Since then, our view has been accepted by some, considered and rejected by others, and (apparently) ignored by others. These developments are discussed at length in chapter 5.

Although we disagree with the revisionist scholars who think that party identification lost much of its importance in the 1970s, our findings are also incompatible with the earlier conventional wisdom associated with researchers at the University of Michigan. The latter difference is less conspicuous because Independents did not occupy such a prominent place in their work. It should be emphasized, however, that none of our findings describes a recent development. With one exception, everything that we say about different types of Independents was as true in the 1950s as it is today. The only difference is the lower level of interest and participation by the genuine Independents, those who deny that they are closer to one party or the other.

Parties in Disrepute

A jaundiced view of political parties is part of our most distinguished intellectual heritage. Parties were, after all, among the most unattractive of those "factions" that the Founding

9. Raymond E. Wolfinger, Martin Shapiro, and Fred I. Greenstein, *Dynamics of American Politics* (Englewood Cliffs, N.J.: Prentice-Hall, 1976), 133, 151.

10. Keith et al., "The Myth of the Independent Voter," paper delivered at the 1977 annual meeting of the American Political Science Association.

Fathers so roundly deplored.[11] Long after parties had become an essential component of the American political system, they were still regarded with suspicion by acute and influential observers. For example, Lord Bryce's model citizen

> will give close and constant attention to public affairs, recognizing that this is his interest as well as his duty. He will try to comprehend the main issues of policy, bringing to them an independent and impartial mind, which thinks first not of his own, but of the general interest. . . . If, owing to inevitable differences of opinion as to what are the measures needed for the general welfare, parties become inevitable, he will join one, and attend its meetings, but will repress the impulses of party spirit. Never failing to come to the polls, he will vote for his party candidate only if satisfied by his capacity and honesty.[12]

Bryce was not alone in urging Americans to keep their distance from parties if they had the astuteness and strength of character to do so. This was the outlook in an 1891 high school civics text:

> As on the playground, some do not care always to go with the crowd, or even prefer to be by themselves. Such as these, who think for themselves, and dare to stand alone, make the Independents in politics.
> They are likely to prefer the good of their country to the success of their party. They will not act with their party, or will leave it, if it is wrong. If the other party changes, as parties sometimes change, and advocates measures that they believe in; if they change their own minds as sensible men sometimes must; or if the other party puts forward better candidates; or if a new party

11. See Austin Ranney, *Curing the Mischiefs of Faction: Party Reform in America* (Berkeley: University of California Press, 1975), 22–57.
12. James Bryce, *Modern Democracies*, vol. 1 (New York: Macmillan, 1929), 47–48.

arises, the independent voters are willing to act wherever they believe they can best secure the public welfare.[13]

In short, partisanship had its place, but it was no substitute for the voter's independence of thought and action. Other students of politics thought that it was up to Independents to rescue the parties:

If the politicians must look after the parties, there should be somebody to look after the politicians, somebody to ask disagreeable questions and to utter uncomfortable truths; somebody to make sure, if possible, before election, not only what but whom the candidate, if elected, is going to represent.... The old parties are not to be reformed from within. It is from without that the attempt must be made, and it is the Independents who must make it. If the attempt should fail, the failure of the experiment of democracy would inevitably follow.[14]

More recently, serious students of politics came to prize parties as an essential part of the polity:

The political parties created democracy and ... modern democracy is unthinkable save in terms of the parties.... The parties are not therefore merely appendages of modern government; they are in the center of it and play a determinative and creative role in it.[15]

Few contemporary political scientists would challenge this view, but most Americans share the Founding Fathers' distaste. In the fall of 1974, in the immediate aftermath of Watergate—a scandal to which neither party contributed— 72 percent of the American public said that the parties were

13. Charles F. Dole, *The New American Citizen* (Boston: D. C. Heath, 1891), 127.
14. James Russell Lowell, "The Place of Independents in Politics," in J. R. Lowell, *Political Essays* (Boston: Houghton, Mifflin, 1888), 318.
15. E. E. Schattschneider, *Party Government* (New York: Farrar & Rinehart, 1942), 1.

the part of the government they "least often trust to do what's right." A mere 13 percent mentioned the president in this connection.[16]

The fundamental explanation for the parties' unpopularity seems to be a belief that they stir up conflict. Jack Dennis, the leading student of the parties' public image, reported that nearly two-thirds of those interviewed agreed that "the political parties more often than not create conflicts where none really exists." Fifty-three percent thought that "our system of government would work a lot more efficiently if we could get rid of conflicts between the parties altogether."[17] In 1980, 56 percent of all NES respondents agreed that "the parties do more to confuse the issues than to provide a clear choice on issues," and just 24 percent dissented from this verdict. Half the sample went so far as to agree that "it would be better if, in all elections, we put no party labels on the ballot."[18]

In view of such sentiments, it is not surprising that the vast majority of Americans deny that a candidate's party is important and insist that they vote for the best candidate, irrespective of party. A month before the 1986 elections, less than 10 percent of registered voters said that the biggest factor in their vote decision would be the candidate's political party.[19]

If party affiliation really influenced the votes of so few people, it would not be the keystone of most efforts in the past thirty-five years to understand voting behavior. We will see that despite their expressions of distaste for the parties, most

16. Unattributed statements about voting and public opinion are based on our analysis of National Election Studies (NES) data. The multi-year tables throughout this book are based when possible on the NES 1952–1988 Cumulative Data File.

17. Jack Dennis, "Support for the Party System by the Mass Public," *American Political Science Review* 60 (September 1966): 605. See also Dennis, "Public Support for the Party System, 1964–1984," paper delivered at the 1986 annual meeting of the American Political Science Association.

18. This item has not been asked of NES respondents since 1980.

19. CBS News–*New York Times* poll release dated October 6, 1986. Nearly three-quarters of the votes cast in the 1986 House elections were along party lines.

Americans are powerfully affected by their affiliations with the Democratic or Republican party.

The Michigan View of Party Identification

Affiliation with a party can be defined in various ways: legal voter registration, formal "card-carrying" membership, or personal identification. The first of these alternatives is a function of state laws, which vary enormously. In some states there is no registration by party; in others, membership is achieved simply by claiming to be a Democrat or Republican when voting in that party's primary. This diversity makes it impossible to use legal registration as the basis of a nationally uniform definition of party membership. The drawback of the second definition, formal membership in an organization, is its rarity; less than 4 percent of all Americans belong to a party in this sense. The third and most useful manifestation of partisanship is party identification, a subjective identification as a Republican or Democrat.

Reporting their analysis of nationwide surveys in 1952 and 1956, four social scientists at the University of Michigan described party identification as the most stable and important determinant of individual voting decisions and the point of departure for analysis of many aspects of public opinion:

> Few factors are of greater importance for our national elections than the lasting attachment of tens of millions of Americans to one of the parties. These loyalties establish a basic division of electoral strength within which the competition of particular campaigns takes place. And they are an important factor in assuring the stability of the party system itself. . . . Most Americans have this sense of attachment with one party or the other. And for the individual who does, the strength and direction of party identification are facts of central importance in accounting for attitude and behavior.[20]

20. Angus Campbell et al., *The American Voter* (New York: John Wiley and Sons, 1960), 121.

The Michigan researchers were not the first to assert that many Americans have durable commitments to a political party. This idea had long been a staple of political commentary and was an important element in the work of such influential scholars as V. O. Key, Jr.[21] But they were the first visible academic survey researchers to identify Republicans and Democrats in other than election-specific terms. Earlier researchers had assigned respondents to a party on the basis of their voting intentions in the impending presidential election.[22] The Michigan contribution in this respect was an operational measure of partisan commitment that was consistent with the previous understanding of this concept, as represented in the work of scholars like Key.

[If party identification were identical to vote choice, it would be an unnecessary term; if it were unrelated to vote choice, it would be without explanatory value. The crux of the concept is that it is antecedent to, distinct from, and influential of individual voting decisions. By conceiving of party identification as an affective attachment, the Michigan scholars made it possible to understand electoral decisions as the interplay of historical forces and such contemporary factors as candidate appeal, disputes about policies, and evaluations of governmental performance.

Few analysts dispute the brilliant simplification involved in the initial Michigan approach, that voting is affected both by long-term predispositions and by short-term cues. Predispositions continue to be much the same from election to election and can be invoked to account for the

21. An especially interesting example is V. O. Key, Jr., and Frank Munger, "Social Determinism and Electoral Decision," in *American Voting Behavior*, ed. Eugene Burdick and Arthur J. Brodbeck (New York: Free Press, 1959).

22. Bernard R. Berelson, Paul F. Lazarsfeld, and William N. McPhee, *Voting* (Chicago: University of Chicago Press, 1954), 25–26. The Gallup Poll began asking about party identification as early as 1937. See Everett Carll Ladd, "Party Identification: The Idea and Its Measure," *The Public Perspective* 2 (May/June 1991): 17.

substantial numbers of electors who always vote for the same party.[23]

An "affective orientation to an important group-object,"[24] party identification was an enduring aspect of the individual's political outlook. It imparted stability, a certain degree of predictability, to elections. Committed partisans—most of the public—were less receptive to candidates appealing to election-year passions. This was nicely illustrated by the pattern of support in 1968 for the third-party presidential candidacy of George C. Wallace, which was based largely on Wallace's hostility to civil-rights laws. These measures were most popular among the young, but so was Wallace, who "captured less than 3 percent of the vote among people over seventy outside the South, but 13 percent of those under thirty, with a regular gradient connecting these two extremes."[25] The explanation for this apparent inconsistency was the strong relationship between age and strength of party attachment. Younger voters, less anchored by party identification, were more vulnerable to Wallace's appeal.

One can easily understand why party identification was not only "the key concept of U.S. electoral research"[26] but also of great interest to a broader scholarly constituency:

> In the course of a mere two decades, party identification has become as pervasive a concept as power, authority, legitimacy, stability, or any other element in the professional political scientist's vocabulary. . . . It offers a

23. Ian Budge, Ivor Crewe, and Dennis Farlie, "Introduction: Party Identification and Beyond," in *Party Identification and Beyond*, ed. Budge, Crewe, and Farlie (New York: John Wiley and Sons, 1976), 18.
24. Campbell et al., *The American Voter*, 121.
25. Philip E. Converse et al., "Continuity and Change in American Politics: Parties and Issues in the 1968 Election," *American Political Science Review* 63 (December 1969): 1103.
26. Michael B. MacKuen, Robert S. Erikson, and James A. Stimson, "Macropartisanship," *American Political Science Review* 83 (December 1989): 1125.

new explanation of democratic stability and legitimacy, which in turn confer authority and power. The more electors are attached by enduring psychological links to political parties, the argument runs, the more the polity is insured against . . . sudden demagogic incursions.[27]

Measuring Party Identification

For more than a generation, social scientists have been identifying Democrats, Republicans, and Independents by asking respondents to apply one of these labels to themselves. The NES uses this question:[28]

Generally speaking, do you usually think of yourself as a Republican, a Democrat, an Independent, or what?

If the respondent answers "Republican" or "Democrat," the interviewer follows up with

Would you call yourself a strong Republican [Democrat] or a not very strong Republican [Democrat]?

If the respondent answers "Independent," the interviewer probes:

27. Budge, Crewe, and Farlie, "Introduction," in *Party Identification*, 3.
28. The NES questions are often used in other academic surveys and by media and political pollsters. The wording ("Generally speaking, do you usually . . .") was designed to encourage respondents to look beyond the immediate present. This contrasts with the Gallup organization's question, which emphasizes the here and now: "In politics, as of today, do you consider yourself a Republican, a Democrat, or an Independent?" Compared to the Gallup measure, responses to the NES question vary much less over time and are considerably less responsive to economic conditions and assessments of presidential performance. See Paul R. Abramson and Charles W. Ostrom, Jr., "Macropartisanship: An Empirical Reassessment," *American Political Science Review* 85 (March 1991): 138–47.
    Gallup seldom uses a probe that permits identification of partisan Independents. For a thoroughgoing review of responses to Gallup questions on party affiliation, see Everett Carll Ladd, Jr., "Declarations of Independents," *Public Opinion*, April–May 1984, 21–32.

Do you think of yourself as closer to the Republican party or to the Democratic party?

⌈Nearly two-thirds of those who initially label themselves Independents concede that they are closer to one or the other party.⌉These are the "leaners," "partisan Independents," or "Independent Republicans" and "Independent Democrats." "Pure Independents" are those who continue to deny any partisan inclinations when asked about closeness to a party⌉ Together with the Strong and Weak ("not so strong") Republicans and Democrats, the NES questions provide seven categories of party identification:[29]

Strong Democrat
Weak Democrat
Independent Democrat
Pure Independent
Independent Republican
Weak Republican
Strong Republican

The full time series from 1952 through 1990, with all seven party identification categories, is in table 1.1.

One obvious decision in any data analysis using the Michigan party identification questions is how to treat respondents who call themselves Independents. Should their initial label be honored? This would create an inclusive category comparable in size to either party's adherents. Or should attention be paid to their response to the probe about closeness to a party? This would produce a small Pure Independent category, less than one respondent in six.

This problem was not mentioned in *The American Voter*'s discussion of measuring party identification, except perhaps for the observation that "by treating Independents as a single

---

29. Once in a while someone identifies with a minor party and a handful of people manifest no interest in parties or politics. These apolitical respondents are discussed in chapters 2 and 9 and will be excluded from data analyses after chapter 2.

Table 1.1 *Party Identification, 1952–1990*

	Strong Democrats	Weak Democrats	Indep. Democrats	Pure Indeps.	Indep. Republicans	Weak Republicans	Strong Republicans	Apolitical
1952	22%	25%	10%	6%	7%	14%	14%	3%
1956	21	23	6	9	8	14	15	4
1958	27	22	7	7	5	17	11	4
1960	20	25	6	10	7	14	16	3
1962	23	23	7	8	6	16	12	4
1964	27	25	9	8	6	14	11	1
1966	18	28	9	12	7	15	10	1
1968	20	25	10	11	9	15	10	1
1970	20	24	10	13	8	15	9	1
1972	15	26	11	13	11	13	10	1
1974	18	21	13	15	9	14	8	3
1976	15	25	12	15	10	14	9	1
1978	15	24	14	14	10	13	8	3
1980	18	23	11	13	10	14	9	2
1982	20	24	11	11	8	14	10	2
1984	17	20	11	11	12	15	12	2
1986	18	22	10	12	11	15	11	2
1988	18	18	12	11	13	14	14	2
1990	17	19	12	11	13	17	11	2

Note: Cross-section samples only; preelection surveys in presidential election years.

group we may reduce seven categories to five."[30] The emphasis was on party identification as "a continuum of partisanship extending from strongly Republican to strongly Democratic."[31] In his article "The Concept of a Normal Vote," Philip E. Converse said that the seven categories of party identification "are often collapsed, as in this article, to five or three classes, in response to needs for greater numbers per class, *or under certain circumstances to assure monotonicity*" (emphasis added).[32]

The authors of *The American Voter* opted to aggregate all Independents for purposes of analysis, setting a precedent that was almost universally observed for nearly twenty years.[33] Independents were the midpoint on a continuum running from Strong Democrats and Weak Democrats to Weak and

30. Campbell et al., *The American Voter*, 123.
31. Ibid., 122–23.
32. Converse, "The Concept of a Normal Vote," 20n.
33. The exceptions to this generalization in the three seminal books by the scholars who conducted the first Michigan studies are sparse enough to be enumerated in one note. The first book from Michigan contained several tables based on the seven-way classification but did not acknowledge in the text that Democratic leaners were more loyal to the Democratic presidential candidate than Weak Democrats or the same pattern on the Republican side. See Angus Campbell, Gerald Gurin, and Warren E. Miller, *The Voter Decides* (Evanston, Ill.: Row, Peterson, 1954), 101, 108–9.

This evident lack of interest in differentiating leaners and Pure Independents continued in *The American Voter*, which presented a great many data analyses that combined all varieties of Independents and just seven tables where they were not combined (pp. 124, 125, 126, 134, 148, 201, 390). Only the tables on pp. 125, 126, and 148 bear on the controversy about how to classify leaners. All three tables show leaners less willing than weak partisans to report a personal history of party regularity. (We discuss this substantive topic and the validity of such retrospective data in chapter 5.)

The single seven-way table in *Elections and the Political Order* (p. 218) concerns one of the few variables that always has a monotonic relationship to strength of party identification: respondents' reports about the partisan consistency of their past voting choices. The same finding appears on p. 125 of *The American Voter*. Another table in *Elections and the Political Order* (p. 197) included leaners with strong and weak partisans in a three-way distribution.

Strong Republicans. Once all three kinds of Independents were in one category, strength of partisanship was positively associated with turnout and other measures of civic virtue, including interest in the campaign and concern about its outcome. The relationship was U-shaped, with Independents at a low point between the partisans of each party. By the same token, the relationship of this five-point measure to vote choice was monotonic. Strong Democrats were most likely to vote for their party's candidate, Weak Democrats less so, then Independents, and so on to the Strong Republicans at the opposite end of the party identification scale.

In sharp contrast to the pre-survey-research view of Independents, *The American Voter* found them ignorant, apathetic, and inactive.[34] Other than impugning their civic virtue, *The American Voter* had little to say about Independents. They were the midpoint on a continuum; their beliefs and behavior were interesting chiefly as a basis of comparison with people of varying degrees of partisan affiliation.

This picture of partisans and Independents became the unchallenged conventional wisdom until the late 1960s when large increases in the number of Independents raised new questions. Although this development led some scholars to characterize Independents in new ways, for some years no one challenged the five-category and three-category scales of party identification that treated Independents as a single group.

The Rise of Independents and the "Decline of the Parties"

In the next few pages we will examine some of the implications that observers of the American political scene have found in the growing number of Independents. Many of these fairly portentous conclusions are associated with explicit rejections of a view of individual political behavior that their authors attribute to *The American Voter*. But both these revi-

34. Campbell et al., *The American Voter*, 143–44.

sionists and the objects of their criticism generally shared the analytic mistake that gave rise to this book: They combined all three kinds of Independents in analyzing data, or they assumed that this combination was appropriate.

We begin with the simple three-way distribution of Democrats, Republicans, and Independents that is commonly used to demonstrate the trend. As fig. 1.1 shows, Independents outnumbered Republicans as early as 1966, became more than a third of the sample in 1972, and first came within two percentage points of the Democrats in 1974. By the end of the 1980s Independents and Democrats had equal proportions of the sample.

The decline of the political parties has of course been a staple item in descriptions of the American political scene for most of this century. In the words of one believer, it is "a frequent refrain among experts in American political parties."[35] The growth in Independents has become an important exhibit in discussion of this putative trend.[36] "While claiming to be an Independent does not necessarily signify a positive commitment to 'Independence,' as a principle, it does reveal a lack of commitment to either of the major parties."[37]

The implications of fewer committed adherents are explicated in this passage from H. G. Nicholas's recent interpretation of American politics:

Indeed one of the most conspicuous features of the contemporary electorate is the growing proportion—

35. Howard L. Reiter, *Parties and Elections in Corporate America* (New York: St. Martin's Press, 1987), 36.
36. See Leon D. Epstein, *Political Parties in the American Mold* (Madison: University of Wisconsin Press, 1986), 4, 240; Nicholas Henry, *Governing at the Grassroots*, 3d ed. (Englewood Cliffs, N.J.: Prentice-Hall, 1987), 111–12; James L. Gibson et al., "Whither the Local Parties? A Cross-Sectional and Longitudinal Analysis of the Strength of Party Organization," *American Journal of Political Science* 29 (February 1985): 139–40.
37. Paul R. Abramson, John H. Aldrich, and David W. Rohde, *Change and Continuity in the 1980 Elections*, rev. ed. (Washington, D.C.: CQ Press, 1983), 240.

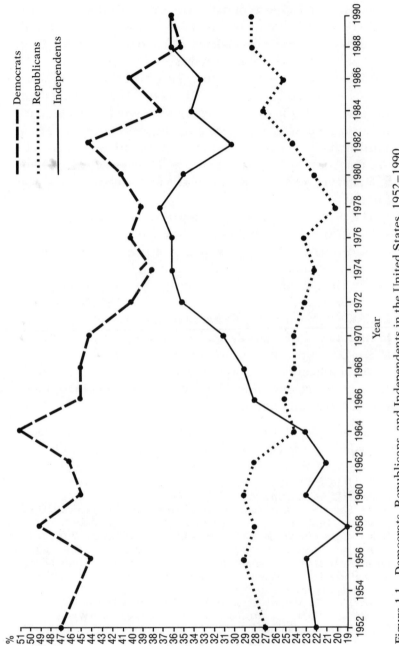

Figure 1.1 Democrats, Republicans, and Independents in the United States, 1952–1990

upwards of 30 percent—which has developed an indifference to party and describes itself as 'Independent.' As such it is unavailable for the day-to-day business of politics, the canvassing, the drumming up of interest in the minor offices, the attendance at meetings, the raising of funds—in short, the maintenance of the structure of participatory politics.[38]

Some writers think that the trend toward more Independents portends not just weaker parties but the end of the party system.[39] One respected scholar has suggested that "if the decline of partisan politics continues, . . . the loss will be that of democracy."[40]

If the proportion of Americans who could be affected by party affiliation was shrinking, it seemed likely that another consequence of the trend would be greater electoral volatility:

Independents operate under no such constraints [as party loyalty]. By definition, their vote (and, for that matter, whether they choose to vote at all) is not anchored by party ties. . . . It is an unstable vote (and turnout) that is basically unpredictable over time, and introduces into elections an increased volatility that today's fluid politics do not need. . . . The independent vote is up for grabs. It has no allegiances. Its volatility and malleability does [*sic*] little to ease the concern of those who value stability and order in American politics.[41]

One casualty of this increased volatility might be effective government. In the opinion of Everett Carll Ladd, Jr., "The

38. H. G. Nicholas, *The Nature of American Politics* (Oxford: Oxford University Press, 1986), 57.
39. Walter Dean Burnham, *Critical Elections and the Mainsprings of American Politics* (New York: W. W. Norton, 1970), 131–34.
40. Gerald M. Pomper, "The Decline of the Party in American Elections," *Political Science Quarterly* 92 (Spring 1977): 41.
41. William J. Crotty, *American Parties in Decline*, 2d ed. (Boston: Little, Brown, 1984), 37. For the same diagnosis of "much wider swings from one election to the next" from a scholar whose political perspective differs from Crotty's, see John H. Kessel, *Presidential Campaign Politics*, 2d ed. (Homewood, Ill.: Dorsey Press, 1984), 279.

fact that a very large proportion of the electorate has been cut loose from relatively stable party ties and has been left free to float necessarily compounds the fragility of the mandate that a modern president enjoys."[42] Hedrick Smith draws a similar conclusion: "This free-floating independence of voters has encouraged the individualism of a new breed of politicians. Since the party brand name lacks the old punch, some candidates run away from their party label when it suits them." Smith goes on to assert that this new breed of politicians with "highly independent campaign styles" is in turn less responsible to party leaders in Congress.[43]

Some writers go beyond characterizing Independents as volatile and see them as something of a bloc.[44] The authors of one textbook observe that "in a strong sense, independents are one of the two major parties."[45] Well-known specialists in voting behavior say that "the large portion of the electorate, mostly young, who have no party ties remains available to

42. Everett Carll Ladd, Jr., *Where Have All the Voters Gone?* 2d ed. (New York: W. W. Norton, 1982), 77.
43. Smith, *The Power Game*, 685, 686.
44. A list of other scholars who combine the three types of Independents for analysis would include Robert C. Luskin, John P. McIver, and Edward G. Carmines, "Issues and the Transmission of Partisanship," *American Journal of Political Science* 33 (May 1989): 444; Carole J. Uhlaner, "Rational Turnout: The Neglected Role of Groups," *American Journal of Political Science* 33 (May 1989): 417; Helmut Norpoth, "Under Way and Here to Stay: Party Realignment in the 1980s?" *Public Opinion Quarterly* 51 (Fall 1987): 385–86; Lee Sigelman et al., "Voting and Nonvoting: A Multi-Election Perspective," *American Journal of Political Science* 29 (November 1985): 757; Charles H. Franklin, "Issue Preferences, Socialization, and the Evolution of Party Identification," *American Journal of Political Science* 28 (August 1984): 469; and Stanley Feldman and Pamela Johnston Conover, "Candidates, Issues, and Voters: The Role of Inference in Political Perception," *Journal of Politics* 45 (November 1983): 824.
45. Kenneth S. Sherrill and David J. Vogler, *Power, Policy and Participation* (New York: Harper and Row, 1982), 317. Sherrill and Vogler also think that "we may be witnessing the disarray and deterioration of *both* parties" (emphasis in original) (p. 282).

attach itself to a new party coalition."[46] Others think the bene-
ficiaries of this big new bloc of potential supporters might not
be limited to the existing two parties. Bruce A. Campbell
wrote that one result of the increase in Independents "is the
advantage that large numbers of Independents present to
third parties. . . . The feeling lingers that sooner or later those
Independents will find a cause around which they can rally."[47]
A few years later, Abramson, Aldrich, and Rohde took the
same line: "The great hope of third parties is the large percentage of the electorate (roughly one-third) who claim to have no
party ties."[48]

[The trend toward independence is believed by some political scientists to be the first step toward partisan realignment,
that is, one or more changes in the profile of identifiers with
the two parties.] At the least, more Independents make such a
reshuffling of party affiliations more feasible: "Since the mid-
1960s, the uncommitted share of the electorate has increased
throughout the nation, thus raising the possibilities for realignment."[49] By the mid-1980s, a historically significant realignment appeared imminent to William Schneider:

> The Democrats are no longer the nation's normal major-
> ity party. That was the big political news of 1984. The big
> question for 1985 is whether the Republicans can take
> their place. One-third of all Americans call themselves
> Republicans, one-third call themselves Democrats and

46. Kenneth Prewitt, Sidney Verba, and Robert H. Salisbury, *Introduction to American Government*, 5th ed. (New York: Harper and
Row, 1987), 359.
47. Bruce A. Campbell, *The American Electorate* (New York: Holt,
Rinehart and Winston, 1979), 268.
48. Abramson, Aldrich, and Rohde, *Change and Continuity*, 237.
49. Paul Allen Beck, "Realignment Begins? The Republican Surge
in Florida," paper delivered at the 1981 annual meeting of the
American Political Science Association, 14; see also Martin P. Wattenberg, "The Hollow Realignment: Partisan Change in a Candidate-Centered Era," *Public Opinion Quarterly* 51 (Spring 1987): 58–
74.

the remaining third are Independents. Is this the long-awaited realignment of American politics?[50]

A more popular interpretation of the trend, however, or a more popular label for it, is "dealignment":

> The present alignment is accompanied, indeed distinguished, by the continued weakening of voter loyalties to political parties in general. I erred four years ago when I argued that the question was whether a realignment or a dealignment was occurring. The larger change in voter alignments we are experiencing includes a greater reluctance on the part of many voters to express any underlying party preference, and an increased willingness to leave the candidate of their professed party with little hesitancy. In general party indentification is a more casual matter than it ever before has been.[51]

The dealignment thesis, which is based on an assumed diminution of the importance of partisanship in voting, is often asserted without support.[52] Advocates of the thesis are among the best-known students of public opinion and voting in America. William Schneider has called it "a major change in American politics."[53] Paul Allen Beck sees the evidence of dealignment as "undeniable."[54] Even Paul Kirk, former chairman of

50. William Schneider, "Demos No Longer the Majority Party," *Los Angeles Times*, December 30, 1984, pt. IV, 1–2.
51. Everett Carll Ladd, Jr., "As the Realignment Turns: A Drama in Many Acts," *Public Opinion*, December 1984–January 1985, 6.
52. James E. Campbell and Joe A. Sumners, "Presidential Coattails in Senate Elections," *American Political Science Review* 84 (June 1990): 513, 520, 521; Edward G. Carmines, John P. McIver, and James A. Stimson, "Unrealized Partisanship: A Theory of Dealignment," *Journal of Politics* 49 (May 1987): 376–400.
53. William Schneider, "Antipartisanship in America," in *Parties and Democracy in Britain and America*, ed. Vernon Bogdanor (New York: Praeger, 1984), 100.
54. Paul Allen Beck, "Incomplete Realignment: The Reagan Legacy for Parties and Elections," in *The Reagan Legacy: Promise and Performance*, ed. Charles O. Jones (Chatham, N.J.: Chatham House, 1988), 165.

the Democratic National Committee, has claimed that "re-alignment is a myth but so-called dealignment is a reality."[55]

An Overview of the Book

Political observers have not been bashful about discerning significance in the apparent diminished importance of party identification. In a few years, Independents were transformed from the forgotten respondents in *The American Voter* into the central characters in a series of melodramatic scenarios about contemporary American politics: electoral volatility, the de-cline of the parties, the loss of governmental authority, the end of the current party system, the birth of third parties, realign-ment, and dealignment. Any or all of these notions may be vindicated by events, but it is important to understand that as of 1991, trends in responses to the NES questions about party identification have not provided much supporting evidence. This is true because researchers who combine all three kinds of Independents when analyzing these data are making a cru-cial mistake. Most respondents who answer the first NES ques-tion by calling themselves Independents are no such thing; as the follow-up question lets us discover, they are covert parti-sans. Therefore, virtually no generalizations about broadly defined "Independents" are correct. Since the interpretations cited in the previous section are based on this mistaken opera-tional definition of Independents, they are wrong. What is true of the revisionist work of the 1970s and 1980s applies equally to the earlier conventional wisdom based on the Michi-gan trilogy.[56]

Some early work about the growth of Independents con-

55. Paul Kirk at the conference "Picking the President: Is There a Better Way?" sponsored by the Public Policy Program and the De-partment of Government, College of William and Mary, Williams-burg, Virginia, November 10, 1989.
56. Campbell, Gurin, and Miller, *The Voter Decides;* Campbell et al., *The American Voter;* Campbell et al., *Elections and the Political Order.*

cluded that it reflected in large measure the Southern shift away from the Democratic party that began in response to the passage of the Civil Rights Act of 1964 and Barry Goldwater's explicit appeal to the South in the election that fall. At the same time, blacks seemed to be moving in the opposite direction from other Americans, becoming more, not less, identified with a party. In chapter 2 we examine regional and racial trends in party identification to ascertain the extent to which blacks and white Southerners differed from the rest of the country.

In the era before survey research, independence was the mark of the ideal citizen. As we have seen, this picture was shattered by *The American Voter*. One part of the revisionist argument challenged this new conventional wisdom, arguing that there were now "two kinds of Independents," one of which was characterized by civic virtue. Chapter 3 shows that neither of these formulations is satisfactory. There are indeed two kinds of Independents: leaners and Pure Independents.

Chapter 4 describes the voting choices of Independents in presidential and congressional elections. It shows that leaners vote very much like the outright partisans of the parties toward which they incline. This finding persuaded many observers that leaners were indeed partisans. Other scholars, however, developed arguments that explained how leaners could vote as they did and still be considered Independents. Chapter 5 deals with this round of responses to our earlier work by examining leaners' participation in presidential primaries, the durability of their party identification, and their views of the two parties.

In chapter 6 we examine the distribution of party identification among people of different ages and educational attainment to test various propositions about the appeal of the parties to different generations and educational groups.

Other, related explanations for the growth of Independents concern the divisive political issues that confronted Americans from 1966 to 1972: Vietnam and race relations. These are the topics of chapter 7. One of the presumed consequences of this pair of issues was widespread disaffection with existing political institutions. In chapter 8, therefore, we examine relations between this phenomenon and party identification.

In chapter 9 we consider two other attempts to explain Independents: that they dislike parties as institutions and that party identification is really a multidimensional phenomenon that was not adequately measured by the Michigan questions. Finally, in chapter 10 we summarize what we have found and examine the implications for diagnoses of the contemporary American political scene.

2

Partisan Shifts among Blacks and Southerners

This chapter has two purposes. First, we show that the increase in Independents was confined to the white population. Overt partisanship spread among blacks while it declined in the white majority. For this reason, most of our analysis in subsequent chapters excludes blacks.

Second, we test the argument that changes in the Southern electorate account for a disproportionately large share of the swelling population of Independents. If this were the case, the South should be discussed separately because any analysis of dealignment using national samples would attribute to the entire country changes that characterized only one region, thus underestimating the regional trend and overestimating the effect everywhere else. We show that the trend toward independence, while evident in the South, is a national phenomenon.

Party Identification among Blacks

For most of American history, black partisanship was of little consequence because most blacks were disfranchised. In the North, where blacks were permitted to vote, their numbers

were modest. In the South, home to most blacks until recently, the end of Reconstruction in the 1870s was followed by
a series of legal and extralegal measures that kept them from
voting in all but a few places.[1] Intimidation dampened other
forms of political expression; many blacks doubtless concluded that it was prudent to treat politics as white people's
business.

In 1940 a mere 3 percent of Southern blacks were registered to vote. A combination of legal pressure and political
mobilization caused a gradual increase in registration, to 20
percent in 1952 and 29 percent in 1960.[2] Over a quarter of
Southern blacks interviewed by the National Election Studies
in 1952, 1956, and 1960 were classified as apolitical; when
asked about their party identification, they denied any affective involvement in politics, even as Independents. Less than
3 percent of Northern blacks and 2 percent of all whites were
apolitical in these three elections. Table 2.1 presents the party
identification of Northern and Southern blacks for the period
1952–1990.[3]

After the Civil War, most blacks identified with the party
whose leader freed the slaves.[4] This historical legacy was
strongest in the South: "From Reconstruction until Franklin
D. Roosevelt, most southern Negroes, insofar as they had parti-

1. See, for example, Charles V. Hamilton, *The Bench and the Ballot*
(New York: Oxford University Press, 1973).
2. Gerald David Jaynes and Robin M. Williams, Jr., eds., *A Common Destiny: Blacks and American Society*, Committee on the Status
of Black Americans, National Research Council (Washington, D.C.:
National Academy Press, 1989), 233. White registration was far
higher, particularly in the Deep South, the last stronghold of the old
tradition that politics was reserved for white people.
3. Rather than the clumsy locution *nonblack*, we will use the
word *white* to describe all respondents who are not black, including
Asian Americans, American Indians, persons of Hispanic heritage,
and other racial minorities. These groups accounted for a substantially larger part of the sample in 1988 than in 1952, but none of
them was numerous enough to permit valid analysis.
4. James L. Sundquist, *Dynamics of the Party System*, rev. ed.
(Washington, D.C.: Brookings Institution, 1983), 219, 347–48.

Table 2.1

Black Party Identification in North and South, 1952–1990

	1952	1956	1960	1964	1968	1972	1976	1980	1984	1988	1990
South											
Strong Democrats	30%	21%	19%	55%	62%	38%	32%	46%	34%	33%	42%
Weak Democrats	21	24	22	21	32	28	37	28	30	26	22
Indep. Democrats	6	3	0	3	0	8	12	6	11	19	13
Pure Independents	1	3	11	8	2	13	11	6	13	5	8
Indep. Republicans	4	1	3	1	0	6	2	5	4	7	6
Weak Republicans	5	8	8	3	0	4	2	1	2	5	4
Strong Republicans	4	10	13	1	2	3	2	4	4	3	3
Apolitical	28	31	25	8	3	1	1	4	2	2	3
	99%	101%	101%	100%	101%	101%	100%	100%	100%	100%	101%
(N) =	(95)	(80)	(79)	(76)	(66)	(141)	(143)	(79)	(137)	(133)	(158)

North

Strong Democrats	32%	34%	29%	49%	51%	35%	37%	44%	31%	44%	37%
Weak Democrats	23	23	16	23	27	34	35	27	33	21	24
Indep. Democrats	15	9	13	14	12	8	17	11	17	17	21
Pure Independents	7	12	20	4	4	10	6	7	8	7	8
Indep. Republicans	3	0	5	0	1	1	1	2	8	4	7
Weak Republicans	12	17	10	8	4	4	3	2	0	5	1
Strong Republicans	5	3	2	3	1	5	1	3	1	0	1
Apolitical	3	2	4	1	4	2	1	4	2	3	1
	100%	100%	99%	102%	101%	99%	101%	100%	100%	101%	100%
(N) =	(74)	(65)	(92)	(80)	(83)	(125)	(147)	(108)	(110)	(134)	(111)

Note: In 1964 and 1968 the black population was oversampled. The black oversample was not included in the analysis. The South is the eleven former Confederate states.

san inclinations, were habitually Republican in the tradition fixed when they had a taste of political power. Eventually Negroes became the only Republicans." The shift toward the Democratic party began with the New Deal. Government intervention on behalf of the deprived moved millions of blacks from the party of Lincoln to the party of Franklin Roosevelt.⁶ As early as 1937, 44 percent of blacks identified with the Democratic party.⁷ By 1952, one of every two blacks was a Strong or Weak Democrat; about one in eight was a Republican.

The climax of the civil rights movement in the mid-1960s accelerated these trends toward full electoral participation and affiliation with the Democratic party. The Voting Rights Act of 1965 provided equal access to the ballot box in the South.⁸ Wholesale repression of black political activity soon became little more than a memory.

The events of 1964 had already modified the two parties' diffuse and ambiguous images on racial issues.⁹ The momentous Civil Rights Act enacted in June of that year was proposed by a Democratic president, passed by a Democratic Congress, and signed into law by another Democratic president. Republican congressmen had been crucial to its enactment, but their hopes of sharing in the credit were lost when their presidential candidate, Senator Barry Goldwater, cast a well-publicized negative vote and then campaigned against the law that fall. Not until 1964 did the Democratic party have the unambiguous image of support for civil rights that has characterized it since then. Nineteen percent of all blacks

5. V. O. Key, Jr., *Southern Politics in State and Nation* (New York: Alfred Knopf, 1950), 286.

6. Nancy J. Weiss, *Farewell to the Party of Lincoln: Black Politics in the Age of FDR* (Princeton, N.J.: Princeton University Press, 1983).

7. Everett Carll Ladd, Jr., and Charles D. Hadley, *Transformations of the American Party System* (New York: W. W. Norton, 1975), 60, 159.

8. Abigail M. Thernstrom, *Whose Votes Count?* (Cambridge: Harvard University Press, 1987), chap. 1.

9. Angus Campbell, "The Meaning of the Election," in *The National Elections of 1964*, ed. Milton C. Cummings, Jr. (Washington: Brookings Institution, 1966), 267–68, and "Civil Rights and the Vote for President," *Psychology Today*, February 1968, 29–30.

had been Strong and Weak Republicans in 1956, as had 16 percent in 1960. This dropped to 7 percent in 1964 and has been below that level since then.

The salience of civil rights in the 1960s and the polarization of the parties' images on those issues raised and clarified for blacks the stakes of electoral conflict. So did their full enfranchisement in the South and the cessation of restraints on their political activity there, which held out the promise of real political power. An obvious consequence of these developments was a much higher level of black political mobilization. One feature of this mobilization was a sharp decline in the number of apolitical Southern blacks—from 25 percent in 1960 to 8 percent in 1964 and then to the same negligible level of Northern blacks and whites everywhere.

A second aspect of black mobilization was an increase in overt identification with one of the two parties; that is, in the proportion of black respondents who said "Democrat" or "Republican" in response to the first question in the NES sequence. Such acknowledged partisans accounted for anywhere from 60 to 69 percent of all blacks from 1952 to 1960. This proportion jumped from 60 percent in 1960 to 81 percent in 1964 and then to a high of 87 percent in 1968. Since then, it has averaged over 70 percent of black respondents.

In 1960, when 27 percent of blacks were Independents, another 14 percent professed no political interest at all. Apolitical black respondents became scarce after 1960. The number of black Independents also declined. Indeed, as fig. 2.1 shows, the 1968 election witnessed the first sharp increase in Independents among whites and another drop among blacks. The rate of black independence more than doubled in 1972, from 10 to 23 percent, but even in that year there were half again as many white Independents.

The clearest conclusion from the trends depicted in fig. 2.1 is that from 1964 onward blacks have been less inclined than whites to call themselves Independents, usually by a substantial margin. Together with the findings about their increasing willingness to identify with a party, this leads us to conclude

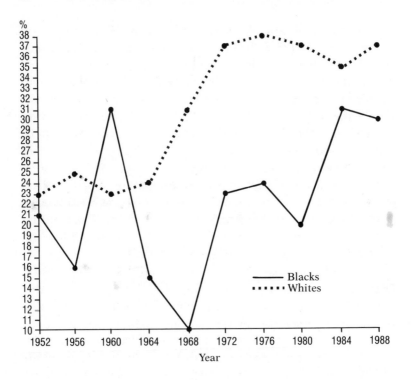

Figure 2.1   Independents by Race, 1952–1988

that for the most part they have not shared in the dealign-ment that is supposed to have begun in the late 1960s. Be-cause blacks have not contributed in full measure to the trend we are examining, we will exclude them from further consid-eration. Unless we specifically indicate otherwise, no data re-ported henceforth include black respondents.[10]

10. Because blacks are the most disaffected of any major popula-tion group, omitting them also avoids complications if one examines relationships between alienation and independence, as we do in chap-ter 8. For a similar decision, see Paul R. Abramson, "Generational Change and the Decline of Party Identification in America: 1952–1974," *American Political Science Review* 70 (June 1975): 469–78.

The South

The direct and immediate consequences of the civil-rights revolution were felt principally in the South: enfranchisement of blacks; the end of Jim Crow laws; legal prohibition of segregated lodging, eating, and entertainment facilities; and great strides toward racial equality. Many Southerners had thought that their familiar way of life required second-class status for blacks. Another part of that way of life had been loyalty to the Democratic party, but the fateful legislation had been signed by a Democratic president. Although Barry Goldwater had forthrightly opposed those measures, the next Republican presidential candidate, Richard M. Nixon, had always been a racial moderate.[11] Hubert H. Humphrey, the Democratic candidate in 1968, was more conspicuously identified with civil rights than any other party leader. This left an opening for a third-party contender: Governor George C. Wallace of Alabama, the country's most famous segregationist. The candidate of the American Independent party, he won 34 percent of all Southern votes and was particularly successful with whites who disliked both Nixon's and Humphrey's stands on civil rights.[12]

In 1971, E. M. Schreiber attributed the nationwide increase in Independents largely to changes in the South.[13] This interpretation had some momentary validity, as can be seen in fig. 2.2, which displays the incidence of independence among white Northerners and Southerners. From 1952 through 1964, the number of Northern Independents was essentially level,

11. Stephen E. Ambrose, *Nixon: The Education of a Politician, 1913–1962* (New York: Simon and Schuster, 1987), 412–14, 433–36, 538, 609.

12. Steven J. Rosenstone, Roy L. Behr, and Edward H. Lazarus, *Third Parties in America* (Princeton, N.J.: Princeton University Press, 1984), 112–14, 163–64.

13. E. M. Schreiber, " 'Where the Ducks Are': Southern Strategy versus Fourth Party," *Public Opinion Quarterly* 35 (Summer 1971): 157–67.

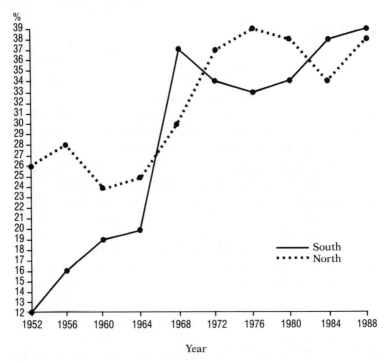

Figure 2.2   White Independents in the North and South, 1952–1988

around a quarter of the sample, and then rose five percentage points from 1964 to 1968. Among white Southerners, on the other hand, Independents increased 17 percentage points from 1964 to 1968. In this last four-year period, white Southerners accounted for more than half the total national increase in Independents.[14]

Between 1968 and 1980, Independents declined in the South and gained elsewhere. Perhaps the Southern highwater mark in 1968 reflected the special circumstances of Wallace's appeal as the candidate of a party that was labeled

14. We define the South as the eleven former Confederate states: Alabama, Arkansas, Florida, Georgia, Louisiana, Mississippi, North Carolina, South Carolina, Tennessee, Texas, and Virginia.

Independent.[15] In any event, from 1972 on, Independents accounted for just over one in three white Southerners and for roughly the same proportion of white Northerners. In 1988, 39 percent of Southern whites were Independents; Northern whites were 37 percent Independent. Because the rise in Independents was a national phenomenon, in no way limited to the South, we include that region in our analysis.

The Democratic party's loss of its monopoly in the South is one of the most significant developments in recent American political history. By the 1980s, Republican presidential candidates fared better in the South than in any other major region. The trend in congressional elections was similar if less dramatic. In the House of Representatives, for example, Southern Republicans held six seats in 1960 and 38 in 1991. Some political scientists attributed these gains not to a broad shift toward Republican affiliation—realignment—but merely to weakening Democratic identification—dealignment. This conclusion was based on the undeniable fact that outright Republican identifiers (Weak and Strong Republicans) were only slightly more numerous among white Southerners in 1972–1988 than in 1960: 21 percent in the earlier year, 24 percent in 1988. Including the leaners as Independents led to such conclusions as these by Paul Allen Beck, author of perhaps the most widely cited study of Southern dealignment:

> Gains in identification with the Republican party in the last two decades have been meager indeed, and the few which appeared through 1960 have been reversed since. . . . GOP prospects for the future seem dim. . . . In short, the future seems bright for neither party. Too large a share of the southern electorate has repudiated party ties. The politics of dealignment are upon the South and should remain dominant for quite some time. . . . Parti-

15. Like other "parties" that are created as vehicles for the presidential campaign of a politician disappointed by his prospects in one of the major parties, the American Independent party faded into obscurity after 1968.

sanship will play a restricted role in the future, just as it has in the past few years.[16]

On the other hand, researchers who classified Independent Republicans as partisans reported a steady increase in Republican identification that led them to conclude that the region was indeed undergoing a realignment.[17] If leaners are combined with outright identifiers with each party, we find that by 1988, 45 percent of all white Southern *voters* were Republicans, compared to 50 percent who were Democrats.

[At this point we anticipate what is to come in this book by reporting that from 1952 through 1984, 92 percent of Southern white Independent Republicans voted for the Republican presidential candidate.] In 1988, Southern Independent Republicans gave George Bush 97 percent of their votes. What is more,

16. Paul Allen Beck, "Partisan Dealignment in the Postwar South," *American Political Science Review* 71 (June 1977): 495. Two other authors who also treated leaners as Independents concluded that the "Republican success in attracting votes [in the South] has been accompanied by failure to secure large numbers of conversions to the party." See Edward G. Carmines and James A. Stimson, "Issue Evolution, Population Replacement, and Normal Partisan Change," *American Political Science Review* 75 (March 1981): 114.

17. See, for example, Raymond E. Wolfinger and Robert B. Arseneau, "Partisan Change in the South, 1952–1976," in *Political Parties: Development and Decay,* ed. Louis Maisel and Joseph Cooper (Beverly Hills, Calif.: Sage, 1978). Although reluctant to accept that leaners are truly partisan and therefore attracted to the "dealignment" label, Earl and Merle Black present data showing the importance of Independent Republicans to partisan changes in the region; see their *Politics and Society in the South* (Cambridge: Harvard University Press, 1987), 239–40.

An article asking how researchers using the same data base could come to such conflicting diagnoses concluded that the answer lay in different choices about "data management" and then had nothing to say about the alternative treatments of Independents that fully explain the conflicting interpretations. See Charles D. Hadley, "Survey Research and Southern Politics: The Implications of Data Management," *Public Opinion Quarterly* 45 (Fall 1981): 393–401. For a thorough survey of the literature on partisan change in the South, see Harold W. Stanley, "Southern Partisan Changes: Dealignment, Realignment or Both?" *Journal of Politics* 50 (February 1988): 64–88.

a growing proportion of votes in the South are cast along party lines. Using our definition of Independents and partisans, Harold Stanley concluded that the evidence pointed to "realignment rather than dealignment insofar as realignment covers an altered balance of partisan identifiers, identifiers remaining loyal in voting, and an increased perception of important, general party differences."[18]

Summary

We have seen that party identification strengthened among blacks at the same time that more whites were becoming Independents. For this reason, our analyses of Independents will exclude blacks. The growth in Independents among whites was a nationwide trend, not a phenomenon whose understanding requires special attention to white Southerners. Finally, our analysis suggests that Republican gains in the South reflect a broad shift toward identification with that party, not merely a weakening of Democratic ties. This conclusion rests on our major theme: The leaners are partisans, not neutrals in the contest between the parties. Chapters 4 and 5 present our case for this conclusion.

18. Stanley, "Southern Partisan Changes," 85.

3

The Civic Virtue of
Partisans and Independents

As we have seen, since the beginning of the Republic, few Americans have been strong admirers of political parties. The rise of corrupt and unresponsive machines after the Civil War provided more reasons for preferring political action that was "prosecuted without the necessarily onerous alliances with political parties."[1] In response to the parties' evident moral squalor, attempts were made to turn them into more satisfactory instruments for political participation. Some thought that this was a futile strategy because the parties were irredeemable. This outlook led to the nonpartisan movement, which generated attempts, with varying degrees of success, to circumvent, subvert, and minimize the parties.

People devoted to nonpartisanship found it easy to believe that independent voters were superior citizens who did not need the crutch of party to make their voting decisions. Howard Penniman nicely summed up this view of party identification: "Faith in the independent voter was thus closely linked to an opposition of intellectuals to political machines—and, indeed, to parties as such. . . . Since the thoughtless ones were

1. M. I. Ostrogorski, *Democracy and the Organization of Political Parties* (London: Macmillan, 1902), 440.

the supporters of the corrupt party machines, then almost by definition the thinking members of society had to become independents."[2]

This belief in the superior civic virtue of Independents was one of the first casualties of survey research, which yielded evidence that Independents were the least likely of any citizens to be interested, informed, and active. The widely accepted epitaph to this ideal was written in *The American Voter:*

> Far from being more attentive, interested, and informed, Independents tend as a group to be somewhat less involved in politics. They have somewhat poorer knowledge of the issues, their image of the candidates is fainter, their interest in the campaign is less, their concern over the outcome is relatively slight. . . . What is more, a further division of the Independent group would show in each case that those who refused to say they were closer to one party or the other are even less involved than other Independents.[3]

The addendum about "a further division of the Independent group" was not elaborated, and few readers seemed to heed it. The harsh verdict on Independents became the new orthodoxy, an application of the generalization that "the stronger the individual's sense of attachment to one of the parties, the greater his psychological involvement in political affairs."[4]

At the beginning of the 1970s, Walter Dean Burnham challenged this conventional wisdom. Burnham noted that some socioeconomic groups with relatively high proportions of Independents were thought to be among the more active and informed parts of the population:

> A new breed of independent seems to be emerging as well—a person with a better-than-average education,

2. Howard Penniman, *The American Political Process* (Princeton, N.J.: Van Nostrand, 1962), 38.
3. Angus Campbell et al., *The American Voter* (New York: John Wiley and Sons, 1960), 143–44.
4. Ibid., 143.

making a better-than-average income in a better-than-average occupation, and, very possibly, a person whose political cognitions and awareness keep him from making identifications with either old party.[5]

It may be entirely likely that there are at least two sets of independents: "old independents" who correspond to the rather bleak classical survey-research picture, and "new independents" who may have declined to identify with either major party not because they are relatively politically unconscious, but because the structure of electoral politics at the present time turns upon parties, issues, and symbolisms which do not have much meaning in terms of their political values or cognitions.[6]

Burnham conceded that this portrait did not include young people and Southerners, who were particularly likely to be Independents.[7] Nor did he actually contrast the civic virtue of Independents and partisans. Nevertheless, his revision of the Michigan position gained considerable acceptance during the 1970s.

Morris Janowitz came to a conclusion very much like Burnham's: "The 'independents' have changed their character and include a high concentration of persons with strong political involvements."[8]

A few years later, Gerald M. Pomper presented another, more empirically grounded defense of Independents. One should not expect them to be particularly concerned or informed about elections and campaigns, he argued, because they have refused to choose sides about these aspects of politics. A more reasonable citizenship test for Independents

5. Walter Dean Burnham, *Critical Elections and the Mainsprings of American Politics* (New York: W. W. Norton, 1970), 130.
6. Ibid., 127.
7. Ibid., 123.
8. Morris Janowitz, "Mass Media: Institutional Trends and Their Consequences," in *Reader in Public Opinion and Mass Communication*, ed. Morris Janowitz and Paul Hirsch (New York: Free Press, 1981), 318.

would focus on topics other than elections fought between Democrats and Republicans. Pomper found that while broadly defined Independents were less informed about the contemporary election than Weak Democrats and Republicans, they surpassed them on questions about public affairs outside the electoral arena.[9]

The conclusions of Burnham, Pomper, and the Michigan scholars all suffer from the same mistake: combining Pure and partisan Independents. Whether the civic virtue of Independents is high, low, or average is a matter of definition. Partisan Independents always have been relatively interested, informed, and active, and Pure Independents have been notably uninterested, ignorant, and inactive. As we will see, however, Pomper's distinction between partisan and other kinds of politics is a useful one.

Interest in Politics

We begin with involvement in activities other than campaigns. Since the 1960s, the Michigan researchers have asked about interest in "what's going on in government and public affairs most of the time, whether there's an election going on or not." Examining the responses across all seven party-identification categories introduces the finding that will recur in this chapter: Pure Independents are at the bottom and partisan Independents at or near the top on measures of political involvement. Table 3.1 shows these data for presidential election years from 1964 to 1988. Pure Independents usually expressed the least interest in politics. Independent Democrats were invariably more interested than Weak Democrats and equaled or surpassed Strong Democrats in five of the seven years. The same is true for Republicans. Independent Republicans were more interested than Weak Republicans in all

9. Gerald M. Pomper, *Voter's Choice* (New York: Harper and Row, 1975), 32–33.

Table 3.1
Party Identification and Interest in Politics, 1964–1988

	Percentage Interested							
	1964	1968	1972	1976	1980	1984	1988	Average 1964–1988
Strong Democrats	72	69	76	79	67	74	63	71
Weak Democrats	64	56	71	68	55	52	57	60
Indep. Democrats	73	71	80	72	67	66	63	70
Pure Independents	65	53	66	60	58	57	43	57
Indep. Republicans	84	84	78	72	65	66	64	73
Weak Republicans	75	63	73	66	62	61	57	65
Strong Republicans	85	72	80	88	79	80	76	80

Note: The entry in each cell is the proportion of respondents in the indicated party-identification category who said they follow politics most or some of the time.

seven years and more interested than Strong Democrats in four of the seven years.

The same pattern appears with respect to two other non-campaign activities—writing letters to editors and to public officials. Pure Independents were the least likely correspondents, followed by weak partisans. Strong partisans and partisan Independents wrote most frequently.

Thus the only Independents out of touch with politics are those who deny any inclination toward a party; that is, about a third of those usually classified as Independents. The partisan Independents are among the most politically involved of all respondents.

What about the argument that partisan Independents, although interested in public affairs, do not care too much about narrow partisan matters like campaigns and elections? They *are* less interested in campaigns than strong partisans but considerably more so than weak partisans. Table 3.2 shows the proportions of each of the seven categories who said they were "very much interested" in the current campaign in every presidential election year from 1952 through 1988. Over this period, Pure Independents usually have been the least interested group. In 1988, for instance, only 14 percent were very interested in the campaign, compared to 24 percent of Independent Republicans and 33 percent of Independent Democrats. Independent Democrats have been at least as interested as Weak Democrats; in seven of the ten election years, they were more interested. The same relationship is found on the Republican side; the mean proportion of Independent Republicans highly interested in the campaign is seven percentage points greater than that of Weak Republicans.

Concern about the election outcome is distributed the same way. Pure Independents were most likely to say they did not "care very much which party wins." Independents who leaned toward either party were generally as concerned as weak partisans and a bit less than strong partisans. At each level of identification, Republicans usually expressed more concern than Democrats.

All these findings suggest that the distinction between campaign and noncampaign politics has no validity for Pure Independents but does reflect variations in the involvement of partisan Independents compared to outright partisans. This might suggest that for partisan Independents, general political interest is weightier than concern about campaigns. Among strong partisans, a larger proportion cares about the election results than displays an interest in politics generally. On the other hand, a relatively higher percentage of partisan Independents are interested in politics than care about the outcome of the party struggle. For outright identifiers, therefore, the campaign may contribute a larger share of the stimuli to their political interest. For partisan Independents, it may be the

Table 3.2

Party Identification and Interest in the Current Election Campaign, 1952–1988

	Percentage "Very Much Interested"										
	1952	1956	1960	1964	1968	1972	1976	1980	1984	1988	Average 1952–1988
Strong Democrats	45	41	46	46	51	42	56	43	47	36	45
Weak Democrats	22	23	27	30	30	24	31	19	21	23	25
Indep. Democrats	43	27	32	29	40	31	31	27	21	33	31
Pure Independents	30	18	27	21	27	20	21	25	17	14	22
Indep. Republicans	43	32	43	39	54	33	34	32	26	24	36
Weak Republicans	34	25	36	34	33	27	32	25	20	22	29
Strong Republicans	62	45	60	57	59	54	64	58	47	46	55

Note: The entry in each cell is the proportion of respondents in the indicated party-identification category who said they were "very much interested" in the current presidential election campaign.

Table 3.3
Party Identification and Knowledge of Congressional Control, 1960–1988

					Percentage Knowledgeable				
	1960	*1964*	*1968*	*1972*	*1976*	*1980*	*1984*	*1988*	*Average 1960–1988*
Strong Democrats	68	67	71	76	70	76	60	64	69
Weak Democrats	65	64	69	60	57	70	53	59	62
Indep. Democrats	64	68	77	59	60	78	59	63	66
Pure Independents	58	55	63	49	50	60	42	47	53
Indep. Republicans	69	78	78	71	68	80	63	64	71
Weak Republicans	72	63	72	68	63	81	56	63	67
Strong Republicans	76	83	77	75	82	85	74	76	79

Note: The entry in each cell is the proportion of respondents in the indicated party–identification category who knew which party had the most seats in Congress before the election.

other way around: general political involvement is what pricks their interest in party politics.

Information

Our findings about levels of political information resemble those about interest in the campaign. Pure Independents are consistently the most ignorant of all Americans. Strong partisans are a bit better informed than leaning Independents, and weak partisans are in third place. These relationships are illustrated by the data in table 3.3, on the extent to which each of the seven groups knew which party had a majority in the House of Representatives before the election in eight presiden-

tial election years. In 1988, for example, only 47 percent of
Pure Independents knew that the Democrats controlled Congress, compared to 63 percent of Independent Democrats and
64 percent of Independent Republicans. In 1984 and 1988,
only Strong Republicans clearly surpassed the two groups of ·
leaners on this question, and Pure Independents were the
least knowledgeable group. The same pattern of differences
between leaners and Pure Independents is found with respect
to respondents' ability to recall the names of candidates for
the House. And in 1976 partisan Independents were more
likely to know if there had been a presidential primary in
their state.

One might think that partisan Independents resemble Burnham's informed, interested "new independents" and that "old
independents" is another label for the sluggish Pure Independents. In fact, the civic virtue of partisan Independents did not
blossom in the fevered political climate of the late 1960s. They
were just as virtuous during the 1950s and did not subsequently become relatively more informed or interested. The
relative levels of concern and information for all party-identification categories have been fairly consistent since the 1950s.
The American Voter's characterization of all Independents as
uninformed about politics and uninterested in the campaign
was true for Pure Independents then and now, but it was never
an accurate portrait of partisan Independents.

Our findings about sharp distinctions among the different
kinds of Independents also explain data that seemingly puzzled other analysts of voting behavior. Examining relationships between "political sophistication" and party identification, Philip Converse thought it "most intriguing" that

> among the most highly sophisticated, those who consider themselves "independents" outnumber those who
> consider themselves "strong" partisans, despite the fact
> that the most vigorous political activity, much of it partisan, is carried on by people falling in this cell. If one
> moves diagonally toward the center of the matrix, this

balance is immediately redressed and redressed very sharply, with strong partisans far outnumbering independents. In general, there is a slight tendency (the most sophisticated cell excepted) for strength of party loyalty to decline as one moves diagonally across the table, and the most "independent" cell is that in the lower right-hand corner.[10]

Converse thought this finding an anomaly. In light of our discussion, it is not surprising to find Independents who are sophisticated about politics—partisan Independents.

Turnout

The most important test of political involvement is voting. The conventional wisdom on this subject was summarized by John F. Bibby:

As the strength of commitment to a party increases, so does the likelihood that a person will turn out and vote. Strong partisans, therefore, have higher rates of turnout than weak partisans, who in turn are more likely to vote than independents.[11]

The evidence for this generalization is a cross-tabulation of turnout and party identification in which all three varieties of Independents are combined. If one compares turnout among all seven party-identification categories, however, it is obvious that turnout is not monotonically related to strength of party identification.

Table 3.4 displays the turnout of the seven categories of party identifiers in presidential elections from 1952 through

10. Philip E. Converse, "The Nature of Belief Systems in Mass Publics," in *Ideology and Discontent*, ed. David Apter (New York: Free Press, 1964), 227.

11. John F. Bibby, *Politics, Parties and Elections in America* (Chicago: Nelson-Hall, 1987), 259. Bibby used the broad definition of Independents.

Table 3.4

Party Identification and Turnout in Presidential Elections, 1952–1988

	1952	1956	1960	1964	1968	1972	1976	1980	1984	1988	Average 1952–1988
							Percentage Who Voted[a]				
Strong Democrats	79	83	85	83	87	79	81	83	86	79	83
Weak Democrats	71	72	78	74	72	73	69	66	70	64	71
Indep. Democrats	80	73	73	73	71	71	73	70	64	69	72
Pure Independents	74	78	75	63	65	53	57	56	61	50	63
Indep. Republicans	82	74	85	85	82	77	74	77	78	66	78
Weak Republicans	80	82	87	84	80	80	74	78	75	78	80
Strong Republicans	94	82	91	92	87	88	93	90	88	90	90

[a]Self-reported turnout.

1988. At each level of strength of identification, Republicans on average vote more than Democrats; the average gap between the two parties is about seven percentage points. Within each party, strong partisans have the highest turnout, about 10 percent more than partisan Independents and weak identifiers. The voting participation of leaners and weak identifiers in each party is similar. The turnout of Independent Democrats has remained constant since 1956, and while voting by Independent Republicans has slackened a bit since their high-water mark in 1960, their turnout is substantially exceeded only by Strong Republicans. As we might expect by now, Pure Independents are the lightest voters. Since 1964, Pure Independents have averaged 11 percent lower turnout than the next-lowest group.[12]

The story is very much the same in midterm contests, as can be seen from table 3.5, which shows turnout in eight recent House elections. The major difference is the tendency of Independent Republicans to vote somewhat less than their fellow Republicans.

These two tables provide no support for the "new breed of Independent" argument. The more interested and knowledgeable segments of the broad Independent grouping, partisan Independents, are no more likely to go to the polls now than they were in the supposedly somnolent Eisenhower years. On the other hand, they are not notably lighter voters now than before. Thus these data are also inconsistent with the notion that the growth of partisan Independents signifies a withdrawal from partisan politics.

12. The data summarized in table 3.4 are for self-reported turnout. Because some respondents falsely claim they voted, the NES now verifies reports about registration and voting by checking county records. This "vote validation" was not done in the early period and has been a consistent practice only in the 1980s; hence our use of self-reported turnout for purposes of continuity. Use of the validated turnout measure for the years in which it is available produces essentially the same pattern as in table 3.4. For instance, the validated turnout for 1988 was Strong Democrat, 73; Weak Democrat, 60; Independent Democrat, 62; Pure Independent, 43; Independent Republican, 60; Weak Republican, 68; Strong Republican, 79.

Table 3.5

Party Identification and Turnout in Midterm Elections, 1958–1990

	Percentage Who Voted[a]									Average 1958–1990
	1958	1962	1966	1970	1974	1978	1982	1986	1990	
Strong Democrats	67	71	71	70	66	71	75	67	64	71
Weak Democrats	51	55	58	55	50	49	60	53	47	55
Indep. Democrats	62	54	53	46	55	53	54	52	39	55
Pure Independents	49	55	46	45	37	40	37	32	28	44
Indep. Republicans	52	59	63	56	56	63	63	56	44	60
Weak Republicans	61	68	68	66	61	64	61	50	46	64
Strong Republicans	78	79	86	79	77	81	80	68	65	79

[a]Self-reported turnout.

The same cannot be said about Pure Independents, how-ever. Until the midsixties, they voted nearly as much as any-one else. In the first three presidential elections in table 3.4, their mean turnout equaled that of Weak and Independent Democrats. Since then, their turnout has fallen off steeply. From the high point of 78 percent in 1956, their voting rate in presidential contests declined almost steadily to 56 percent in 1980, fully 10 percentage points below any other class of iden-tifier. Although Pure Independents' turnout rose to 61 percent in 1984, it remained well below that of either group of leaners. In 1988 only half the Pure Independents voted, 14 percent below the next-lowest category.

The decline in Pure Independents' turnout vitiates the elec-toral impact of their growing numbers. In 1956, 9 percent of all presidential-election voters (including blacks) were Pure Independents. As table 3.6 shows, this proportion remained remarkably constant in the ensuing thirty-four years. In 1988, 7 percent of all voters in the presidential election were Pure Independents. For the period 1956–1988, the average propor-tion of all presidential voters who were Pure Independents was 9 percent.

The same is true in both presidential-year and midterm elections for the House. This is why we have avoided talking about increasing numbers of independent *voters*. This finding should put a damper on speculations about a larger and larger pool of uncommitted voters who are "up for grabs" in election campaigns. As we shall see, Pure Independents are the only Independents who fit this description, and they con-tribute the same share of the total vote now that they did in the 1950s.[13]

13. The stable proportion of Pure Independents in the voting population also disposes of James L. Sundquist's attempt to shrug off our earlier work by pointing out that "all three categories of independents have grown as a proportion of the electorate, so limit-ing the term to the nonleaning independents would not alter the interpretation in this chapter." See his *Dynamics of the Party System*, rev. ed. (Washington, D.C.: Brookings Institution, 1983), 397n.

Table 3.6
Percentage of All Voters Who Were Pure
Independents, 1956–1990

	Presidential Elections	Midterm Elections
1956	9	
1958		6
1960	9	
1962		7
1964	6	
1966		9
1968	9	
1970		10
1972	9	
1974		10
1976	11	
1978		10
1980	10	
1982		6
1984	9	
1986		7
1988	7	
1990		6

Note: This table includes all voters, including blacks,
who said they went to the polls, irrespective of
whether they cast a ballot in a particular contest.

Participation in Campaigns

Campaign activity other than voting calls for greater commitment and more energy. In his attempt to rehabilitate Independents' reputation for civic virtue, Pomper conceded that "in
regard to electoral politics, Independents do show less activity and do conform to the accepted description of limited
involvement."[14] The most widespread type of campaign activ-

14. Pomper, *Voter's Choice*, 32.

ity is trying to talk someone into voting for a candidate. Predictably, Pure Independents have been least likely to do this. It comes as something of a surprise, however, to learn that Weak Democrats are frequently as inactive. In the middle are Independent Democrats, Independent Republicans, and Weak Republicans, surpassed by Strong Democrats, Independent Republicans, and—most active of all—Strong Republicans. Pomper's conclusion (which accurately described the "accepted position") is true only for Pure Independents; leaners are much more like partisans than Pure Independents in their level of campaign involvement.

The same is true for the less common forms of electioneering: financial contributions, attendance at meetings, and other activities helpful to candidates and parties. Because a small proportion of the population does any of these things, we created a participation index by combining all three types of behavior. The results for ten presidential elections are presented in table 3.7. Perhaps because of the relatively small number of cases in any cell, the numbers jump around a bit; nevertheless, the outlines are clear. The familiar pattern appears again: Republicans are more active than Democrats, strong partisans are most active, and Pure Independents are least active. In either party, leaners and weak partisans are about equally likely to participate in the campaign.

These campaign activities are seldom performed in an organizational or emotional vacuum. They are the sorts of things that party activists do and in fact are usually the identifying signs of party organization membership.[15] The relatively high level of such behavior by partisan Independents is yet another reason to question the customary assumption that they are without party ties. So is the finding that fully 30 percent of the delegates to the 1972 Democratic National Convention identified themselves as Independent Democrats. The counter-

15. See, for example, David Nexon, "Asymmetry in the Political System: Occasional Activists in the Republican and Democratic Parties, 1956–1964," *American Political Science Review* 65 (September 1971): 716–30.

Table 3.7

Party Identification and Campaign Activity, 1952–1988

	Percentage Who Gave Money, Went to a Meeting, or Otherwise Worked in the Campaign										Average 1952–1988
	1952	1956	1960	1964	1968	1972	1976	1980	1984	1988	
Strong Democrats	10	20	19	13	19	17	22	13	21	13	17
Weak Democrats	5	13	9	9	9	11	16	8	10	8	10
Indep. Democrats	14	13	11	8	15	15	14	8	10	14	12
Pure Independents	9	8	11	5	10	7	14	6	8	5	8
Indep. Republicans	9	15	17	15	13	13	19	12	10	10	13
Weak Republicans	9	14	19	18	13	17	15	20	11	13	15
Strong Republicans	18	21	33	42	31	24	39	30	21	23	28

Note: The entry in each cell is the proportion of respondents in the indicated party identification category who performed at least one of the three listed activities.

part identity was claimed by 12 percent of the Republican delegates in 1972.[16]

Previous Findings

The relationships reported in this chapter have not gone wholly unnoticed in the literature. Indeed, the first book by the Michigan group contained tables showing that partisan Independents voted and participated more than weak partisans.[17] This finding was not acknowledged in the text, however. As we said earlier, the data analyses presented in *The American Voter* did not generally separate Pure and partisan Independents. Robert Cantor remarked on the nonmonotonic relationship between party identification and general political interest. But he seemed interested primarily in attacking the importance and validity of the whole notion of party identification, and the thrust of his argument went in that direction.[18] Theodore J. Macaluso reported, "Somewhat surprisingly in light of the conventional wisdom . . . leaning Independents appear to be the most informed segment of the electorate."[19] Warren E. Miller and Teresa E. Levitin noted that leaners vote more than weak partisans and "seem to be among the most well-informed, involved, issue-oriented of citizens. . . . The Independent Inde-

16. Joseph H. Boyett, "Background Characteristics of Delegates to the 1972 Conventions: A Summary Report of Findings from a National Sample," *Western Political Quarterly* 27 (September 1974): 477.

17. Angus Campbell, Gerald Gurin, and Warren E. Miller, *The Voter Decides* (Evanston, Ill.: Row, Peterson, 1954), 101, 108–9. For another early report of the same finding, see Robert Agger, "Independents and Party Identifiers: Characteristics and Behavior in 1952," in *American Voting Behavior*, ed. Eugene Burdick and Arthur J. Brodbeck (New York: Free Press, 1959), 319–20.

18. Robert D. Cantor, *Voting Behavior and Presidential Elections* (Itasca, Ill.: Peacock, 1975), 37.

19. Theodore J. Macaluso, "Political Information, Party Identification, and Voting Defection," *Public Opinion Quarterly* 41 (Summer 1977): 257–58.

pendents are, in contrast, predominantly disinterested nonparticipants in political affairs.[20]

John Petrocik made the most elaborate analysis of the relationship between partisanship and civic virtue that appeared before our 1977 paper.[21] He began by noting that contrary to expectation, many measures of interest and activity were not monotonically related to party identification. Pointing out that these behaviors were also related to differences in education, income, and direction of partisan choice, Petrocik argued that if one wanted to isolate the effect of partisan affiliation on civic virtue, it was necessary to control for the other independent variables. Controlling for education, income, and Republican affiliation reduced or reversed the apparent advantage of partisan Independents over weak partisans. Petrocik concluded that the familiar index of party identification was problematic.

Our interest, however, is different from Petrocik's. We are concerned not with the relative importance of different independent variables as explanations of political involvement but with the election-level and systemic issues raised in chapter 1. None of these issues is affected by the undisputed finding that independent variables other than party identification help explain civic virtue. In short, we seek to characterize Independents, not to explain political activity.

Petrocik did not discuss the most interesting aspects of party identification—its relationship to various measures of partisan choice—except to observe that "the measurement of party identification given to the profession by the [Michigan] Survey Research Center is useful for explaining the phenomenon for which it was designed; it adequately accounts for party-specific attitudes and behaviors."[22] The evident ratio-

20. Warren E. Miller and Teresa E. Levitin, *Leadership and Change: Presidential Elections from 1952 to 1976* (Cambridge, Mass.: Winthrop, 1976), 99.
21. John R. Petrocik, "An Analysis of Intransitivities in the Index of Party Identification," *Political Methodology* 1 (Summer 1974): 31–47.
22. Ibid., 41.

nale for this verdict was Petrocik's belief that "while weak identifiers are partisans, leaners are basically independents."[23] We
will consider the evidence for this assertion in the next two
chapters.

John C. Pierce and Paul R. Hagner, writing after our findings were first presented, found the same difference between
Pure Independents and leaners. Compared to leaners,

> The pure independents exhibit a much higher propor-
> tion of no-issue orientations and a lower proportion of
> ideologues. This pattern is repeated in each of the six
> elections. . . . It is only this pure classification of indepen-
> dents which fits the description of having low interest
> and awareness of electoral politics.[24]

Some scholars have attempted to explain variations in turnout by means of multivariate analysis in which leaners and
Pure Independents are combined.[25] Others, in our opinion
more wisely, have combined leaners and weak partisans.[26]
Dealignment, "whose most obvious manifestation is the growing proportion of Independents,"[27] has been nominated as a
prime cause of falling turnout:

> The behavioural consequences of dealignment include
> increasing voter apathy, growing volatility, and greater

23. Ibid., 35.
24. John C. Pierce and Paul R. Hagner, "Conceptualization and
Party Identification: 1956–76," *American Journal of Political Science*
26 (May 1982): 384. See also Herbert B. Asher, *Presidential Elections
and American Politics*, 4th ed. (Chicago: Dorsey Press, 1988), 86–87,
115–17.
25. Lee Sigelman et al., "Voting and Nonvoting: A Multi-Election
Perspective," *American Journal of Political Science* 29 (November
1985): 749–65; Carole J. Uhlaner, "Rational Turnout: The Neglected
Role of Groups," *American Journal of Political Science* 33 (May 1989):
390–422.
26. Paul R. Abramson and John H. Aldrich, "The Decline of Electoral Participation in America," *American Political Science Review* 76
(September 1982): 502–21.
27. William Schneider, "Antipartisanship in America," in *Parties
and Democracy in Britain and America*, ed. Vernon Bogdanor (New
York: Praeger, 1984), 100.

Table 3.8

Change in Presidential Election Turnout from the 1960s to the 1980s, by Party Identification

	Average Turnout, 1960–64–68[a]	Average Turnout, 1980–84–88[a]	Decline
Strong Democrats	85	83	2
Weak Democrats	75	67	8
Indep. Democrats	72	67	5
Pure Independents	68	56	12
Indep. Republicans	84	73	11
Weak Republicans	84	77	7
Strong Republicans	90	89	1[b]

[a]The entry in each cell is the weighted average of the corresponding cells in table 3.4.
[b]All entries have been rounded; the actual difference for Strong Republicans is 0.4 percent.

interest in unconventional political alternatives. It is well known that Independents exhibit these characteristics and that the proportion of Independents has been growing steadily since 1964.[28]

We have condensed some of the data from table 3.4 in table 3.8 to enable readers to assess more easily this proposition from William Schneider, based on the broad-spectrum definition of Independents. It is accurate regarding Pure Independents. They have become more numerous and have been voting at a much lower rate than in the sixties. As for the leaners, however, their aggregate turnout decline is matched by that of weak partisans. The two categories—partisan Independents and weak partisans—appear to be equal contributors to falling turnout.

28. Ibid., 114.

Summary

There is a wide disparity in the political interest and involvement of Pure and partisan Independents. Pure Independents are consistently the least interested, informed, and active of any partisan classification. Partisan Independents, in contrast, are not only more interested and involved than Pure Independents but as, or more, interested and involved than weak partisans. This was as true for the 1950s as the 1980s. The only notable change over this period has been a decline among Pure Independents, who display even less civic virtue now than they did a generation earlier.

4

How Independents Vote

The Michigan measure of party identification reflects the extent to which individuals consider themselves Democrats, Republicans, or Independents. The most useful and powerful application of this identity is in voting decisions. The importance of party identification to the political system comes from the combination of its relationship to vote choice and its persistence from one election to the next. As Nie, Verba, and Petrocik put it, "A voter with no party identification cannot vote on the basis of party. Thus the growth in the number of Independents automatically reduces the number who can give a party vote."[1]

Because they have nothing to be loyal to, it has been argued that Independents respond more freely than partisans to the short-term forces of the campaign, the candidates and issues that provide the dynamic element in elections. If nearly 40 percent of all Americans are "simply and tautologically unconstrained by partisanship,"[2] it is easy to see why the decline of

1. Norman H. Nie, Sidney Verba, and John R. Petrocik, *The Changing American Voter*, enlarged ed. (Cambridge: Harvard University Press, 1979), 157.
2. Gerald M. Pomper, *Voter's Choice* (New York: Harper and Row, 1975), 40.

partisan affiliation has led many observers to predict fundamental political change (see chapter 1). On the other hand, if
this description applies only to the much smaller number of
Pure Independents, then the threat to political stability posed
by the increasing numbers of Independents has been vastly
exaggerated.

Do leaners vote like outright partisans or like Pure Independents? This simple question was not directly answered in *The
American Voter*, which introduced the concept of party identification and established the analytic categories that guided political scientists' use of that concept. The questions that elic-
ited each respondent's "partisan self-image" made it possible
for "us to place each person in these [1952 and 1956] samples
on a *continuum* of partisanship extending from strongly Republican to strongly Democratic."[3] The impression of a monotonic
relationship between party identification and vote choice suggested by this quotation was reinforced by passages like this:

> The effect of party [on vote choice] is seen at once in the
> changing location of the distributions [of the probability
> of voting for the Republican presidential candidate in
> 1956] along this probability dimension as we consider
> successively Strong Democrats, Weak Democrats, Inde-
> pendents, Weak Republicans, and Strong Republicans.[4]

This refers to a multivariate analysis of the relationship
between a cluster of attitudes and the presidential vote. On
the next page is a simple cross-tabulation of the presidential
vote in 1952 and 1956 with the five-point classification of
party identification usually employed in *The American Voter*,
combining all three varieties of Independents.[5] Fig. 4.1 repro-
duces this cross-tabulation for 1956. It shows a smoothly
monotonic decline from Strong Democratic to Strong Repub-

3. Angus Campbell et al., *The American Voter* (New York: John
Wiley and Sons, 1960), 122–23, emphasis added. For the questions,
see pp. 12–13 above.
4. Campbell et al., *The American Voter*, 138.
5. Ibid., 139. See note 33, chapter 1.

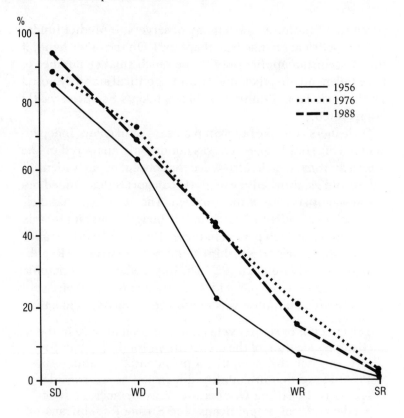

Figure 4.1   Five-Point Party Identification and Vote for
Democratic Presidential Candidate, 1956, 1976, and 1988

lican in the share of the vote received by Adlai Stevenson in
his rematch with Dwight D. Eisenhower. We also plotted in
fig. 4.1 the same relationship in 1976, a Democratic year when
Jimmy Carter edged out Gerald R. Ford and for 1988, when
George Bush defeated Michael Dukakis. These lines are even
straighter than the one representing Stevenson's vote from
each of the five party-identifier categories.

When they introduced their measure of party identification, the authors of *The American Voter* discussed the possibility that many self-designated Independents might really be
covert partisans:

Sometimes it is said that a good number of those who call themselves Independents have simply adopted a label that conceals a genuine psychological commitment to one party or the other. . . . We have incorporated in our measure of party identification a means of distinguishing Independents who say they lean toward one of the parties from Independents who say they do not. We do not think that the problem of measurement presented by the concealed partisan is large. Rather it seems to us much less troublesome than the problems that follow if psychological ties to party are measured in terms of the vote.[6]

Dismissal of fears about covert partisans masquerading as Independents was justified after analysis of responses to this question: "Have you always voted for the same party or have you voted for different parties for President?"[7] The proportion of respondents who said they always or mostly voted for the same party went from 82 percent of strong party identifiers and 60 percent of weak identifiers to 36 percent of leaners and a mere 16 percent of Pure Independents. Even more striking results were achieved by dividing the sample at age 35 to control for younger voters' fewer opportunities to opt for different parties. After presenting these data, Campbell and his associates concluded that "we will describe relatively few genuine partisans as Independents by using self-classification to measure party attachments."[8]

As we will show in this and the following chapter, this is a defensible conclusion only if leaners are excluded from the Independent category. Before starting to demonstrate this, the central proposition in this book, let us examine briefly the candidate preferences of Pure Independents. One would predict that lacking any party to which they could be loyal, they would be more susceptible to influences specific to each elec-

6. Campbell et al., *The American Voter,* 123, 125.
7. Ibid., 125.
8. Ibid., 125–26, quoted passage at p. 126. We discuss the inadequacy of such retrospective data in chapter 5.

tion: current issues, the appeal of that year's candidates, and judgments on the administration's performance. This is why the putative increase in Independents moved observers to anticipate wider and wider swings from one election to the next—in a word, volatility.

Volatility is the right word for Pure Independents' voting patterns. Fig. 4.2 depicts the percentages of white Pure Independents and of all white respondents who voted for the Democratic presidential candidate in every election from 1952 through 1988. As a general proposition, the Pure Independent vote reflects in an exaggerated way the election outcome. Candidates who win by a landslide take an even more lopsided share of the Pure Independent vote. When Lyndon B. Johnson crushed Barry Goldwater with 65 percent of all votes cast by whites in 1964, he received 75 percent of the Pure Independent vote. Both numbers were about the same in Richard M. Nixon's one-sided victory over George McGovern in 1972. Eisenhower's appeal to Pure Independents was even more disproportionate when he defeated Stevenson with 55 percent of the total vote in 1952 and 58 percent four years later. In 1980, when Ronald Reagan had a 5:4 advantage over Jimmy Carter in the popular vote, he won among Pure Independents by a 3:1 ratio, 66 to 22 percent (John Anderson took the other 12 percent). In closer elections, Pure Independents usually vote for the winner (1976 was an exception), but not by very much. George Wallace's candidacy muddied the waters in 1968 when he won 18 percent of Pure Independent votes, compared to 13 percent of the total popular vote.

The sharp peaks and deep troughs in fig. 4.2 leave no room for doubts about Pure Independents' volatility. We have already seen, however, that they amount to less than 10 percent of voters in presidential elections, a proportion that has remained essentially unchanged since the 1950s (see table 3.6, p. 52). If there is any justification for the fears of so many political scientists that we are in an era of heightened electoral instability, it must lie in the behavior of partisan Independents, who are responsible for most of the growth in the

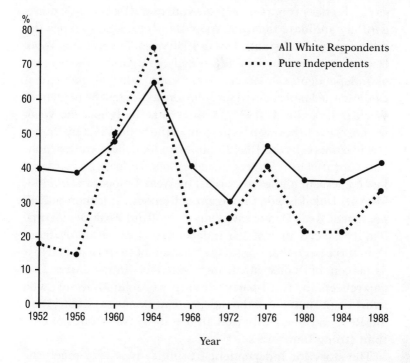

Figure 4.2   Vote for Democratic Presidential Candidate of Pure Independents and All White Respondents, 1952–1988

inclusive Independent category and account for two-thirds of all Independents. The conventional wisdom, and the root cause of all the worry about partisan instability, is that Independents "are not guided by a party affiliation."[9] As we have just seen, this seems a fair description of Pure Independents' voting practices.

Leaners are a very different story. They display an impressive tendency to vote for the candidate of the party they feel closer to; indeed, in presidential elections *they are generally more loyal to their party than weak partisans.* In seven of the ten

9. Nie, Verba, and Petrocik, *The Changing American Voter,* 50.

presidential elections since 1952, Independent Democrats gave a higher proportion of their vote to the Democratic presidential candidate than did Weak Democrats. Sometimes the difference was substantial, as in 1960 when 71 percent of Weak Democrats voted for John F. Kennedy, compared to 86 percent of Independent Democrats. Four years later, 89 percent of Democratic leaners voted for Johnson, as against 81 percent of Weak Democrats. In 1972, McGovern actually lost the Weak Democrat vote but won 58 percent of the ballots cast by Democratic leaners. In the 1984 Republican landslide, Walter Mondale captured fully 76 percent of Democratic leaners' votes and just 63 percent of the ballots cast by Weak Democrats. In 1988, Michael Dukakis won 88 percent of Democratic leaners and 67 percent of Weak Democrats. Only in 1980 did Weak Democrats' loyalty exceed that of the Independent Democrats by more than three percentage points; 53 percent of the former and just 41 percent of Democratic leaners voted for Jimmy Carter. This gap reflects the third-party candidacy of John Anderson, who won fully 20 percent of the Independent Democratic vote. Ronald Reagan ran equally well among these two groups of less-than-strong Democrats.

The story for Independent Republicans is very much the same. They exceeded Weak Republicans in party loyalty by a considerable margin in two years, 1964 and 1976. On average since 1952, 89 percent of Independent Republicans have voted for the Republican presidential candidate, compared to 87 percent of Weak Republicans. Only in 1980 when 11 percent of them voted for Jimmy Carter, compared to just 5 percent of Weak Republicans, were they significantly less loyal. On average, both groups of leaners were more likely than their counterpart weak identifiers to vote for their party's candidate.

Patterns of party-line voting among Southern whites are somewhat different. All three varieties of Southern Republicans are very loyal. In the past nine presidential elections, fully 98 percent of Strong Republicans voted for their party's candidate, as did 92 percent of Independent Republicans and 91 percent of Weak Republicans. In 1984, every white Southern Independent Republican in the NES sample voted for

Reagan. They were just as likely as Weak Republicans to vote for Republican House candidates and more likely to choose the Republican Senate candidate. Among white Southern Democrats, on the other hand, only strong identifiers consistently back their party's presidential candidates, and even they vote 8 percent less Democratic on average than their Northern counterparts. The other two groups of Southern Democrats are more likely than not to defect. Weak identifiers are more loyal than leaners, who nevertheless vote for Democrats much more than do the Pure Independents.[10]

These findings about the voting behavior of independent leaners are a spectacular refutation of the orthodox belief that party regularity is proportionate to strength of party identification. The extent of the damage is illustrated by fig. 4.3 where we have plotted the same relationship between party identification and vote for the Democratic presidential candidate shown in fig. 4.1, but with one alteration: Party identification is now measured by a seven-point rather than five-point scale. The result is dramatic; the nearly straight parallel trend lines in fig. 4.1 are transformed, in fig. 4.3, into jagged strokes that move in an irregular stair-step pattern across the page.

Table 4.1 also sheds light on another commonplace assertion about contemporary political life: the alleged diminishing relevance of party identification to the decision Americans make on election day. For example, Marjorie Randon Hershey had this to say:

Although most voting-age Americans still express a psychological attachment to one of the major parties, that attachment has weakened and means less and less in elections. . . . Party has less influence on people's voting choices than it once did; . . . the parties, quite simply, are becoming irrelevant to large numbers of Americans.[11]

10. Raymond E. Wolfinger and Michael G. Hagen, "Republican Prospects: Southern Comfort," *Public Opinion* 8 (October–November 1985): 8–13.
11. Marjorie Randon Hershey, *Running for Office* (Chatham, N.J.: Chatham House, 1984), 24.

Table 4.1

Party Identification and Vote for Democratic Presidential Candidates, 1952–1988

	Percentage Who Voted for the Democratic Presidential Candidate											Vote for Wallace, 1968	Vote for Anderson, 1980
	1952	1956	1960	1964	1968	1972	1976	1980	1984	1988	Average[a]		
Strong Democrats	82	85	90	94	80	66	88	83	87	93	85	7	6
Weak Democrats	61	62	71	81	54	44	72	53	63	67	63	14	8
Indep. Democrats	59	65	86	89	50	58	70	41	76	88	67	17	20
Pure Independents	17	15	49	75	22	25	41	21	22	32	31	18	12
Indep. Republicans	7	7	13	25	4	12	14	11	5	14	11	13	10
Weak Republicans	5	7	11	40	9	9	21	5	6	16	13	8	9
Strong Republicans	2	1	2	9	3	2	3	4	2	2	3	2	4

[a]Average of annual percentages.

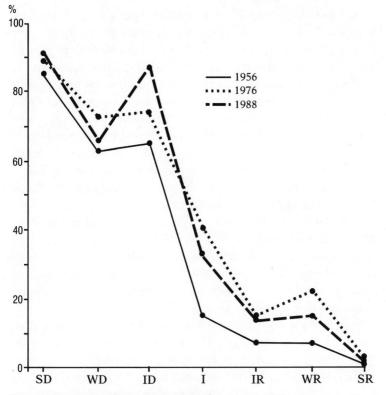

Figure 4.3   Seven-Point Party Identification and Vote for
Democratic Presidential Candidate, 1956, 1976, and 1988

William Crotty's view of the importance of party identification is even more negative about

> an increasing disparity between [party] identification
> and the vote. There is an increasing willingness on the
> part of many party members to break with their party
> and its candidates and to vote for the opposition. . . . the
> odds are not much over fifty-fifty today that a party identi-
> fier will vote for his party's presidential nominee. Repub-
> licans are little different from Democrats in this regard.[12]

12. William Crotty, *American Parties in Decline*, 2d ed. (Boston:
Little, Brown, 1984), 31, 34.

Against these sweeping generalizations we contrast table 4.1, which shows that in the ten-election period from 1952 through 1988 there was no significant increase in defection by any of the six party-identifier categories. Other than simple inspection, this also can be seen by computing each category's average Democratic vote for the three elections of the 1980s and comparing that number to the mean for the previous seven elections. The difference between the two numbers is two or fewer percentage points in three of the six cases. Defection increased by three percentage points among Weak Democrats and declined by about the same amount among Weak Republicans and Strong Democrats.

The data in table 4.1 are no kinder to Crotty's proposition about the similarity in the party loyalty of Democrats and Republicans in presidential elections. Simply put, in nine of the past ten elections, Democrats have been substantially more prone to defect. (This has not been the case in House elections, as we will see shortly.)

The finding that leaners display more party loyalty than weak partisans strikingly illustrates our basic proposition that leaners are partisan, not neutral. Although a nonmonotonic relationship of the kind shown in table 4.1 and fig. 4.3 is a particularly arresting demonstration of our thesis, it is not the appropriate criterion. We will see that leaners do not always match or exceed weak identifiers on all measures of partisan affect, but *they are never neutral, and the extent of their affect almost invariably resembles that of weak partisans.*

These remarks introduce our findings on voting in House elections, which show little nonmonotonicity but consistent party-line voting by leaners. Table 4.2 displays how the seven categories of white identifiers voted in the fifteen House elections from 1962 through 1990. Comparison with table 4.1 reveals that Independent Democrats were *more* loyal in House than in presidential voting; 74 percent were party-line voters in House elections, compared to 67 percent when voting for president. But Weak Democrats were much more loyal when voting for Congress, so much so that over the twenty-eight-year period, they were slightly stronger party voters in House races than the leaners were. A closer look at table 4.2 shows that this difference was found mostly in the 1960s. Beginning in 1972, Independent Democrats equaled or surpassed Weak Democrats in party-line voting in every House election year but two. In 1978, 79 percent of Weak Democrats and only 60 percent of leaners voted for Democratic congressional candidates. Even with this deviant year included, Democratic leaners have been faintly more loyal in these ten elections: 77 percent, compared to 75 percent for Weak Democrats.

[Compared to Democrats, Republicans defect less in presidential elections and more when voting for the House] This reflects the pull of incumbency and the much greater number of Democratic incumbents. Even so, Republican leaners choose their party's House candidates by about a 2:1 ratio; Weak Republicans are five percentage points more loyal. Better-informed voters are more likely to defect in House elections, which may explain why leaners desert their parties more than the less-informed weak identifiers.[13]

The discovery that leaners are slightly less loyal than weak identifiers in House elections gave heart for a time to defenders of the old view that leaners are not partisans. At the beginning of the 1980s, John R. Petrocik drew this conclusion:

> The "biased" Independents [that is, leaners] appear rather partisan only in their presidential choices. In other contests Independents are much less likely to support the candidate of the party toward which they lean than are the weak identifiers.[14]

13. Thomas E. Mann and Raymond E. Wolfinger, "Candidates and Parties in Congressional Elections," *American Political Science Review* 74 (September 1980): 621–22.

14. John R. Petrocik, *Party Coalitions* (Chicago: University of Chicago Press, 1981), 159. See also his "Contextual Sources of Voting Behavior: The Changeable American Voter," in *The Electorate Reconsidered*, ed. John C. Pierce and John L. Sullivan (Beverly Hills, Calif.: Sage, 1980), 265–66.

At the end of the decade, Petrocik reported that data from 151 surveys conducted for congressional, state, and local candidates

Table 4.2
Party Identification and Vote for Democratic House Candidates, 1962–1990

| | Percentage Who Voted for the Democratic House Candidate | | | | | | | | | | | | | | |
	1962	1964	1966	1968	1970	1972	1974	1976	1978	1980	1982	1984	1986	1988	1990	Average[a]
Strong Democrats	96	93	93	88	91	91	89	86	83	81	90	87	91	87	90	89
Weak Democrats	83	84	81	72	76	79	80	76	79	66	74	66	71	80	79	76
Indep. Democrats	74	78	55	61	74	79	85	76	60	68	84	76	72	86	79	74
Pure Independents	61	71	49	48	50	54	53	55	56	57	30	59	58	66	61	55
Indep. Republicans	27	28	33	18	35	27	37	32	37	32	36	39	37	37	32	32
Weak Republicans	14	35	22	21	17	24	32	28	34	26	20	34	34	30	39	27
Strong Republicans	6	8	12	8	5	15	14	15	19	22	12	15	19	23	17	14

[a]Average of annual percentages.

It is difficult to reconcile this conclusion with leaners' degree of party-line voting; 74 percent of Independent Democrats and 33 percent of Independent Republicans vote for Democratic House candidates. We see no reason to ignore this gap, deny that leaners are partisan, and combine them in an omnibus Independent category that mingles three distinct types of voters.

The partisanship of leaners was reported in the literature before we presented our findings in 1977. Some scholars presented tables or charts depicting the nonmonotonic relationship but then failed to mention it in the text.[15] William Flanigan and Nancy Zingale, however, did draw the appropriate conclusion:

> On crucial attitudes and in important forms of political behavior, the "leaning" independents appear quite partisan. Independents who lean toward the Democratic party behave rather like weak Democratic partisans, and the same is true on the Republican side. . . . independent

---

showed this pattern of voting for Republican candidates: 33 percent by Weak Democrats, 36 percent by Independent Democrats, 71 percent by Independent Republicans, and 75 percent by Weak Republicans. The multivariate analysis on which the study was based "separates independents into three groups: two groups of leaners and those who insist they have no preference for either party." See his "An Expected Party Vote: New Data for an Old Concept," *American Journal of Political Science* 33 (February 1989): 44–66, quoted passage at 53.

Two years earlier, he had written that "all data referring to Democrats and Republicans are based on a definition of partisanship which includes strong, weak, and leaning identifiers as partisans." See his "Realignment: The South, New Party Coalitions and the Elections of 1984 and 1986," in Warren E. Miller and John R. Petrocik, *Where's the Party? An Assessment of Changes in Party Loyalty and Party Coalitions in the 1980s* (Washington, D.C.: Center for National Policy, 1987), 54n.

15. Robert D. Cantor, *Voting Behavior and Presidential Elections* (Itasca, Ill.: Peacock, 1975), 34; Peter B. Natchez and Irvin C. Bupp, "Candidates, Issues, and Voters," in *Political Opinion and Behavior*, 2d ed., ed. Edward C. Dreyer and Walter A. Rosenbaum (Belmont, Calif.: Wadsworth, 1970), 447.

leaners are more interested in campaigns than are weak partisans, and they are as likely to vote and even as likely to be loyal to "their" party as are weak partisans.[16]

Having said this, they proceeded in the rest of this edition of their book to analyze data combining all three types of Independents.

Warren Miller and Teresa Levitin clearly described the leaners' partisan voting habits:

> In fact, between 1952 and 1976 the two groups of Independent leaners voted more solidly in support of their party preferences than did weak identifiers in almost all of the several electoral opportunities to do so. This persistent partisan behavior on the part of self–designated Independents raises questions about the meaning of the self–classification.[17]

> However, there is too little research on the political perceptions, evaluations, and behaviors of Independent leaners to answer these questions.[18]

Miller and Levitin concluded that the leaners' voting patterns suggested that "the simple fact of an increase in the incidence of Independents cannot be taken as evidence of a decline in the importance of partisanship."[19] Few scholars or other observers heeded this prudent warning. Another passage from Miller and Levitin seemed more consistent with most interpretations of the last two decades: "Since they are not tied to a party and respond primarily to the short–term issue and candidate forces of each particular election, the

16. William H. Flanigan and Nancy H. Zingale, *Political Behavior of the American Electorate*, 6th ed. (Boston: Allyn and Bacon, 1987), 46.
17. Warren E. Miller and Teresa E. Levitin, *Leadership and Change: Presidential Elections from 1952 to 1976* (Cambridge, Mass.: Winthrop, 1976), 210.
18. Ibid., 252.
19. Ibid., 210.

Independent leaners are also a relatively volatile segment of the electorate."[20]

Since the late 1970s, many specialists in voting behavior have acknowledged the partisan character of leaners. This shift is so far from universal, however, that even scholars as well informed as Robert L. Lineberry and George C. Edwards II could write in 1989:

> For most white Americans, though, party desertion— the abandonment of either party for a nonparty attachment—is well advanced. This abandonment occurred at all age levels in the electorate, though it was more pronounced for those with the weakest party ties, that is, younger voters.[21]

In the next chapter we consider various reactions to the finding that leaners vote like outright partisans and then examine a variety of other evidence that sheds light on the central question: Are they really neutral, or are they committed to the party toward which they lean?

20. Ibid., 99.
21. Robert L. Lineberry and George C. Edwards II, *Government in America*, 4th ed. (Glenview, Ill.: Scott, Foresman, 1989), 252. Lineberry and Edwards relied on Gallup data that showed 28 to 33 percent of Americans were Independents in the 1970s and 1980s.

5

Partisans or Independents?

The discovery that most leaners are loyal party voters called into question the prevailing view of party identification. By the beginning of the 1980s, study of this topic, once a model of consensus, was marked by controversy and confusion. Some scholars accepted our interpretation of leaners' voting behavior: They vote as they do because they are more partisan than independent—not neutral, but nearly as committed to a party as those who readily acknowledge their affiliations. Analyses using all seven party-identification categories, once scarce, became commonplace.[1]

1. Media and political pollsters dealt with the topic in various ways. As early as 1976, the CBS News–*New York Times* polls divided leaners and Pure Independents. *Newsweek* and the NBC–Associated Press surveys did this during the 1980 election season. One advantage of this practice was realized in the 1980 preconvention period: classifying leaners as partisans made it easier for pollsters to accumulate enough cases for analysis of intraparty candidate preferences.

Richard Wirthlin, President Ronald Reagan's pollster, reported, "We find that when people say they are independent, and then we ask them which party they lean toward, they are stronger partisans than many of those who declare a party." Quoted in Elizabeth Drew,

Not everyone accepted these distinctions, however. A surprising number of scholars did not seem aware that it was important to differentiate between leaners and Pure Independents. Experienced students of elections continued to produce variations on the "partisanship is dying" theme:

Independents have increased markedly in number to the point where they now rank in some polls as equal to or slightly behind the Democrats and well ahead of the Republicans. The day is not far off when independent will clearly be the identification preferred by most Americans. In fact, there is nothing to indicate a substantial reversal or leveling off of the trend shown. Thus, independents will most likely continue to increase in significance and number with each passing election year. From an electorate in which 75 percent of its members loyally associated themselves with the major parties to one (in future elections) in which the majority may well claim to be independents is a major transition that, in itself, has changed, and will continue to change, the practice of American politics.[2]

"A Political Journal," *The New Yorker*, February 20, 1984, 116. See also Wirthlin, "Partisan Change in the 1980s: A Rolling Realignment," *The Public Perspective* 1 (November–December 1989): 14.

For some years after 1980, however, the Gallup organization still did not ask about leaning—or did not report the results if it did ask—and so continued to report that over 30 percent of all Americans were Independents. A Gallup release in the spring of 1983 appeared under this headline: "Republican Affiliation Falls to 1 in 4," *San Francisco Chronicle*, March 10, 1983, 13.

2. The short and long quotations are both from William Crotty, *American Politics in Decline*, 2d ed. (Boston: Little, Brown, 1984), 42, 28–30. Like some other scholars with his point of view, Crotty presented tables showing differences between leaners and Pure Independents that he ignored in the text.

For other examples of the same theme, see Paul R. Abramson, John H. Aldrich, and David W. Rohde, *Change and Continuity in the 1980 Elections*, rev. ed. (Washington, D.C.: CQ Press, 1983), 237; William J. Keefe et al., *American Democracy: Institutions, Politics, and Policies* (New York: Harper and Row, 1990), 237; Everett Carll Ladd, Jr., *Where Have All the Voters Gone?*, 2d ed. (New York: W. W. Norton, 1982), 77–78, 124; Kevin P. Phillips, *Post-Conservative America* (New York: Random House, 1982), 227–28; Kenneth Prewitt and Sidney Verba, *An Introduction to American Government*, 4th ed. (New York:

In a lead editorial during the 1980 campaign, the *New York Times* said that the one-third of the population who initially called themselves Independents could be indicative of

> a large and growing corps of voters located between the major parties [who might provide support for] an independent movement, a Center Party, a Third Force, made up of people unsatisfied with both sides of a Carter-Reagan race, and fastening mostly on John Anderson.[3]

In addition to the converted and the apparently oblivious, there was a third category: the explicit skeptics, scholars who knew that there are two ways of looking at Independents but nevertheless carried on with the old way. The skeptics often relied on various interpretations of leaners' voting choices that preserved the conventional wisdom, but some did not seem to think it necessary to justify their orthodoxy. Charles H. Franklin, for example, after noting that "some recent research has questioned" the old assumption of monotonicity, announced (without benefit of argument or citation), "I prefer to retain it."[4] Other skeptics, however, did

---

Harper and Row, 1983), 392–93, 400, 402; and James L. Sundquist, *Dynamics of the Party System*, rev. ed. (Washington: Brookings Institution, 1983), 394–408.

3. The *New York Times*, March 20, 1980, A26. Readers will notice that the *New York Times* and Abramson and his collaborators have been on both sides of the dispute about Independents.

In the middle of 1983, John Anderson was reported to believe that the "one-third" of the population who "claim no ties" to a party provided an opportunity for a third-party movement; George F. Will, "Is a Third Party Necessary?" *Newsweek*, May 23, 1983, 88. A year later, the *Washington Post*'s director of polling wrote that the "between 35 and 40 percent" of American adults who "considered themselves independents . . . appear to present fertile ground for the kind of effort Anderson says he is willing to undertake"; Barry Sussman, "Why Anderson's Third-Party Bid May Hit Responsive Chords," *Washington Post* (national weekly ed.), May 21, 1984, 37.

4. Charles H. Franklin, "Issue Preferences, Socialization, and the Evolution of Party Identification," *American Journal of Political Science* 28 (August 1984): 469.

explain their adherence to the traditional position that leaners should not be considered party identifiers. Perhaps the
most comprehensive, if compressed, statement is Warren E.
Miller's:

> Although it is true that the so-called Independent Demo-
> crats and Independent Republicans may behave very
> much as partisans in the short-term, even outdoing
> weak identifiers in the homogeneity of their voting
> partisanship—they are more volatile in their partisan-
> ship over the long-term; and, when tested by measures
> of their psychological ties to the parties, they are de-
> monstrably the independents they claim to be, more
> moved by candidates or issues and less identified with
> their preferred party of the moment.[5]

In this chapter we test explanations of leaners' voting
choices that preserve the conventional wisdom about their
essential neutrality.[6] We employ a variety of measures other
than voting choice that shed light on the basic question: How
partisan are the leaners? We will answer this question by
describing their participation in presidential primaries, the
stability of their voting choices and party identification, and
their assessment of the two parties.

---

5. Warren E. Miller, "Party Identification Re-examined: The Reagan Era," in Warren E. Miller and John R. Petrocik, *Where's the
Party? An Assessment of Changes in Party Loyalty and Party Coalitions
in the 1980s* (Washington, D.C.: Center for National Policy, 1987),
24n. Neither data nor citations were presented to support this conclusion. For a more theoretically grounded defense of the traditional
position, see Miller, "Party Identification, Realignment, and Party
Voting: Back to the Basics," *American Political Science Review* 85
(June 1991). We will consider this argument near the end of this
chapter.
6. As we observed in the previous chapter, some writers found
support for their belief in the leaners' nonpartisanship in the finding
that they were faintly less loyal than weak partisans in voting for
House candidates. See, for example, William Schneider, "Antipartisanship in America," in *Parties and Democracy in Britain and America*, ed. Vernon Bogdanor (New York: Praeger, 1984), 116–17.

Participation in Presidential Primaries

American political theory and practice have provided several definitions of party membership. All are plausible, and none is conclusive.[7] The major practical implication of these endless legal, political, and scholarly controversies is eligibility to vote in party elections. Primaries have usually been considered reforms that weakened the parties as institutions because voters rather than party leaders choose nominees. But Leon D. Epstein argues that at the individual level, primaries necessarily strengthen partisanship because they "must encourage voters to think of themselves as Republicans or Democrats."[8] This point is particularly important for independent partisans. If their designation of a party to which they are closer is nothing more than a signal of their intentions in the general election, one would expect them to be under no impulsion to participate in one or the other party's primary. What is more, because most states have registration by party and closed primaries, choosing a primary to vote in cannot be a spur-of-the-moment decision.

For both of these reasons, we can learn something about the stable partisan identifications of leaners by looking at their participation in presidential primaries when competition for the nomination was stiff in both parties. One such year was 1980; 38 percent of the NES sample who lived in a state with a presidential primary in 1980 reported voting in that primary.[9] Leaners were as likely as weak partisans to

7. See Austin Ranney, *Curing the Mischiefs of Faction* (Berkeley: University of California Press, 1975), 147–69.

8. Leon D. Epstein, *Political Parties in the American Mold* (Madison: University of Wisconsin Press, 1986), 246. Epstein cites a study by Steven E. Finkel and Howard A. Scarrow that shows a relationship between registration by party and more partisan responses to the party-identification question; see their "Party Identification and Party Enrollment: The Difference and the Consequence," *Journal of Politics* 47 (May 1985): 620–42.

9. For similar findings about the 1976 presidential primaries, see Keith et al., "The Partisan Affinities of Independent 'Leaners,'" *British Journal of Political Science* 16 (April 1986): 165–66.

Table 5.1

Participation in Presidential Primaries, 1980 and 1988

| | 1980 | | 1988[a] | |
	Percentage voting in a presidential primary	Percentage voting in their party's primary	Percentage voting in a presidential primary	Percentage voting in their party's primary
Strong Democrats	54	97	52	98
Weak Democrats	36	92	38	97
Indep. Democrats	35	76	33	95
Pure Independents	18	—	20	—
Indep. Republicans	36	70	28	76
Weak Republicans	36	87	33	81
Strong Republicans	65	97	46	98

[a]In 1988 the question asked about participating in a primary or, in caucus states, a presidential nominating caucus.

participate; just over a third of both groups voted, with no difference between Democrats and Republicans. This was double the turnout rate of Pure Independents. Asked which party's primary they had participated in, 76 percent of Independent Democrats said they had voted in the Democratic contest, compared to over 90 percent of the other two types of Democrats. The corresponding figures on the Republican side were 70 percent for leaners, 87 percent for weak partisans, and 97 percent for the strong partisans. These data are in table 5.1, which includes the counterpart findings for 1988.

In 1988, 36 percent of the sample reported voting in a presidential primary or caucus. In both parties, leaners' turnout rate was five percentage points below that of weak partisans. As before, Pure Independents were much the least active, and strong partisans the most active. Participation in the Democratic primary ranged from 98 percent by Strong Democrats to an almost identical rate of 95 percent by Independent Democrats. Seventy-six percent of Republican leaners chose to participate in a Republican primary; Weak Republicans were a mere five percentage points more likely to do so.

We can summarize our findings as follows: Leaners are not notably more reluctant than weak partisans to participate in presidential primaries. When it comes to choosing one or the other party's primary, the four possible comparisons in 1980 and 1988 yield three different findings. In one case, that of 1988 Democrats, leaners were almost unanimous participants in their party's primary. In two other cases, the odds were better than three to one that a Democratic leaner in 1980 and a Republican leaner in 1988 would pick his or her party's primary. The weakest case for our general theme is the 1980 Independent Republicans, of whom "only" 70 percent voted in the Republican primary.

More evidence in support of our argument comes from Gary D. Wekkin's study of voting in the 1980 presidential primaries in Wisconsin, where citizens may choose to participate in either party's primary. He found that weak and leaning Democrats and Republicans were equally likely to vote in their respective party's primary. "What Keith et al. found to be true of independent-leaning voting behavior in general elections may also hold true in presidential primaries."[10] We interpret Wekkin's finding and our own as evidence that when respondents say they are closer to a party they are revealing an enduring identity more than a response to passing issues and personalities.

10. Gary D. Wekkin, "The Conceptualization and Measurement of Crossover Voting," *Western Political Quarterly* 41 (March 1988): 112.

The Stability of Party Identification

⌈The essence of party identification is "some engagement of partisan feelings with self-identity."[11] Few people redefine themselves frequently; hence self-definition implies stability.⌋ Something closely resembling enduring party identification is also implicit in the presurvey-era studies based on analysis of election returns that characterized particular regions or groups as partisan for reasons attributed to distant historical experience: eastern Tennessee, blacks before the New Deal, Catholics. The acquisition of party affiliation by children in advance of any political understanding and the transmission of party identification from parents to children also suggest stable partisan orientations.[12] The role of party identification in the "edifice" of thinking about political perceptions, beliefs, and choices associated with *The American Voter* assumed that it was fairly stable:

> In the period of our studies [1952 and 1956] the influence of party identification on attitudes toward the perceived elements of politics has been far more important than the influence of these attitudes on party identification itself.[13]

Defining party identification as a long-term predisposition made it possible to ascertain the importance in a given electoral setting of more ephemeral factors such as the candidates' appeal, issues, and evaluations of governmental perfor-

---

11. Philip E. Converse and Roy Pierce, "Measuring Partisanship," *Political Methodology* 11 (1985): 144. The other element they consider "absolutely central to the whole notion of party identification: an extended time horizon."

12. Fred I. Greenstein, *Children and Politics* (New Haven: Yale University Press, 1965), chap. 4; M. Kent Jennings and Richard G. Niemi, *The Political Character of Adolescence* (Princeton, N.J.: Princeton University Press, 1974), chap. 2.

13. Angus Campbell et al., *The American Voter* (New York: John Wiley and Sons, 1960), 135.

mance. The elections of the 1950s seemed well suited to this analytic goal. The Republicans gained the White House because millions of Democrats voted for Dwight Eisenhower without changing party or (particularly after 1952) voting in equal measure for Republican congressional candidates.

While all these findings were consistent with the proposition that party identification was a relatively stable variable, they did not directly measure stability. The same was true of the similar distributions of party identification that were observed in the nationwide survey data that the Michigan researchers began to accumulate at two-year intervals after 1956 (see table 1.1). It could be argued, however, that the impressive aggregate stability in those repeated cross sections could conceal considerable shifting among the various categories of party identification. There were two ways to explore stability directly. One was to ask respondents if there was "ever a time when you thought of yourself as a Democrat (Republican) rather than a Republican (Democrat)?" As we will see shortly, this is not a valid way to measure change in party identifications.

The second method is through a "panel study," repeated interviews with the same sample over a period of years. Panel studies are very expensive, subject to considerable attrition, and likely to produce a preternaturally informed and interested sample of survivors. The Michigan researchers have incorporated a panel design in their nationwide electoral research only twice—in the 1956–58–60 period and in 1972–74–76. This summary of the results from the first panel applies equally to the second one: "the stability of party identifications in the 1956–60 period vastly outstripped the stability of individual positions on even the most stable of the major political issues of the period."[14]

14. Philip E. Converse and Gregory B. Markus, "Plus ça change ... : The New CPS Election Study Panel," *American Political Science Review* 73 (March 1979): 33. The standard study of the comparative stability of party identification and political attitudes in the 1952–54–56 panel is Philip E. Converse, "The Nature of Belief Systems in

Such comparisons did not directly address the stability of party identification, a topic that was not illuminated in print until the 1970s, when one could learn that nearly one in six respondents in the earlier panel had moved from one to another of the three major groups—Democrat, Pure Independent, or Republican—and that less than 60 percent of the sample had given the identical response to the party-identification questions in any two-year period. Instability was slightly higher in 1972–74–76.[15]

If party identification had changed so much, what was causing it to do so? Studies began to appear showing that partisanship was influenced by various contemporary phenomena, including evaluations of the presidential candidates,[16] assessments of presidential performance,[17] respondents' comparisons of their own issue preferences and those they attributed to the parties,[18] vote intentions in the current election,[19] and appraisals of current economic conditions.[20] These had all been considered responsive to party identification, endogenous variables in models of vote choice. Party identification

Mass Publics," in *Ideology and Discontent*, ed. David Apter (New York: Free Press, 1964), 206–61.

15. Morris P. Fiorina, *Retrospective Voting in American National Elections* (New Haven: Yale University Press, 1981), 87–88. For a summary of the earlier studies of change in party identification, see Fiorina, pp. 86–89.

16. Benjamin I. Page and Calvin C. Jones, "Reciprocal Effects of Policy Preferences, Party Loyalties, and the Vote," *American Political Science Review* 73 (December 1979): 1071–89.

17. Fiorina, *Retrospective Voting;* Michael B. MacKuen, Robert S. Erikson, and James A. Stimson, "Macropartisanship," *American Political Science Review* 83 (December 1989): 1125–42.

18. Franklin, "Issue Preferences"; John E. Jackson, "Issues, Party Choices, and Presidential Votes," *American Journal of Political Science* 19 (April 1975): 161–85; Charles H. Franklin and John E. Jackson, "The Dynamics of Party Identification," *American Political Science Review* 77 (December 1983): 957–73.

19. Gregory B. Markus and Philip E. Converse, "A Dynamic Simultaneous Equation Model of Electoral Choice," *American Political Science Review* 73 (December 1979): 1055–70.

20. MacKuen, Erikson, and Stimson, "Macropartisanship."

had been treated as an "unmoved mover," an exogenous variable. Now it appeared that the relationship might well run as powerfully in the opposite direction, indeed that party identification was little more than an amalgam of the individual's reaction to contemporary events and conditions. This is how some defenders of the conventional wisdom had explained leaners' partisanship; now the suggestion was extended to all categories of party identifier.[21]

This interpretation probably went beyond the intentions of the scholars cited in the previous paragraphs, although one can find support for it here and there, particularly in Fiorina's book, which attacked the conventional wisdom with exceptional clarity, force, and color. His reduction of party identification to "a running tally of retrospective evaluations" seemed more memorable than his "disclaimer" that some people "may never forget Hoover's depression or Sherman's march to the sea," which carried retrospective evaluation to a previously unimagined historical dimension.[22]

The entire literature alleging the instability of party identification has been challenged on methodological grounds by Donald Philip Green and Bradley Palmquist, who argue that the imprecision of survey instruments calls into question both apparent changes in party identification and responsiveness of partisanship to short-term forces.

> The problem of response error has been largely ignored in recent models of partisan change. As a result, estimates that purport to show the lability of party identification with respect to candidate evaluations, voting behavior, issue proximities, and performance evaluations turn out to be statistical artifacts. In retrospect, it would appear that in their enthusiasm for the use of sophisticated non-

---

21. Some of these studies classified leaners as partisans when defining the variables in their models; others adhered to the traditional wide-spectrum view of Independents. None of them, however, shed any light on whether leaners were particularly susceptible to short-term forces.

22. Fiorina, *Retrospective Voting*, 94, 91.

recursive estimation techniques, researchers in this area have tended to lose sight of the inherent deficiencies of survey data.[23]

One source of the measurement error discussed by Green and Palmquist is suggested by Converse and Roy Pierce:

> Citizens marginal to the electoral process, for example, such as chronic non-voters, give responses to the party identification item which are very unstable and which seem to move dynamically in tune with whatever party the respondent would vote for at the moment (assuming interest enough to get to the polls, which is usually absent).[24]

The controversy about the stability of party identification in general sets the stage for our consideration of leaners' stability. Some political scientists do not think that leaners' indisputably partisan voting habits are inconsistent with the conventional wisdom. They consider leaners not hidden Democrats and Republicans but neutrals who decide how to vote and then use that decision when answering the question about which party they are closer to. "Since I'm going to vote for Dukakis, I guess I'm closer to the Democrats."

We continue our appraisal of this interpretation by comparing the stability of different categories of identifiers. The first data source is the repeated interviews of the 1972–1976 panel in the Michigan NES. We plotted the full array of 1972 respondents according to their identification in 1976, thus producing a seven-by-seven matrix of partisan affiliation. This revealed considerable movement from category to category.[25]

23. Donald Philip Green and Bradley Palmquist, "Of Artifacts and Partisan Instability," *American Journal of Political Science* 34 (August 1990): 899. The MacKuen, Erikson, and Stimson study was the only one cited above not criticized in detail by Green and Palmquist.

24. Converse and Pierce, "Measuring Partisanship," 150.

25. Including respondents' party identification in 1974 would increase the sense of movement since some respondents who were in the same partisan category in 1972 and 1976 were somewhere else in 1974.

Relatively few of these changes were from one party to the other, however; most were shifts in the intensity of partisan identity, not in its direction. The overwhelming majority of people who professed some affiliation with a party in 1972 were still on that side four years later. We will call these respondents *directionally stable.* Many others shifted only to the Pure Independent category, leaving a handful who crossed the divide from one party to the other. This latter group is the *directionally unstable.* The proportions of different categories of identifiers in the directionally stable and unstable groups are shown in table 5.2.

Table 5.2
Stability of Party Identification

	Directionally Stable[a]			Directionally Unstable[b]		
	1972–76	*1965–73*	*1973–82*	*1972–76*	*1965–73*	*1973–82*
Strong Democrats	95	94	96	3	4	3
Weak Democrats	85	80	91	8	13	6
Indep. Democrats	79	72	75	12	10	9
Indep. Republicans	63	77	73	15	13	15
Weak Republicans	88	80	88	6	10	9
Strong Republicans	92	90	96	6	4	3

SOURCES: We computed the 1972–1976 and 1965–1973 data. The data for 1973–1982, which include black respondents, are from Jennings and Markus, "Partisan Orientations over the Long Haul," 1005. The 1965–1973 and 1973–1982 comparisons are for the parental generation only.

a The percentage of respondents in the indicated party identification category in the earlier year who still identified with the same party (as strong, weak, or independent partisans) four, eight, or nine years later.
b The percentage of respondents in the indicated party identification category in the earlier year who identified with the other party (as strong, weak, or independent partisans) four, eight, or nine years later.

As we might expect, strong partisans were the most stable; 95 percent of 1972 Strong Democrats and 92 percent of Strong Republicans were on the same side of the fence in 1976. They were not far ahead of weak partisans, however; 85 percent of Weak Democrats and 88 percent of Weak Republicans were directionally stable. Independent Democrats were scarcely less fixed in their partisan identity than Weak Democrats; 79 percent were directionally stable. The same could not be said for Republican leaners; "only" 63 percent of them were directionally stable. The remainder did not become Democrats, however, as a glance at the "directionally unstable" column in table 5.2 reveals. Just 15 percent of Republican leaners crossed to the other party. The gap on the Republican side between leaners and outright partisans is nine percentage points, which is scarcely overwhelming. To put it another way, the chances that an Independent Republican would be driven into Democratic ranks by Watergate and other shocks of the years from 1972 to 1976 are less than one in six.[26] The directional instability of Democratic leaners is a bit lower, and scarcely higher than that of Weak Democrats: 12 percent as opposed to 8 percent.

Another source of data on change in party identification is a national sample of high school seniors and their parents who were interviewed in 1965, in 1973, and a third time in 1982.[27]

---

26. Richard A. Brody has shown that the events of 1973 and 1974 were associated with shifts away from Republican identification; see his "Stability and Change in Party Identification: Presidential to Off-Years," in *Reasoning and Choice: Explorations in Political Psychology*, ed. Paul M. Sniderman, Richard A. Brody, and Philip E. Tetlock (New York: Cambridge University Press, 1991).

27. The first wave of interviews was reported in Jennings and Niemi, *The Political Character of Adolescence*, the first two waves in Jennings and Niemi, *Generations and Politics* (Princeton, N.J.: Princeton University Press, 1981). Some results from the third wave may be found in Jennings and Gregory B. Markus, "Partisan Orientations over the Long Haul: Results from the Three-Wave Political Socialization Panel Study," *American Political Science Review* 78 (December 1984): 1000–1018. Of the 1,562 parents in the original sample in 1965, just 898 were interviewed in 1982 (p. 1001).

This provides much more time for change than the 1972–1976 panel. The disadvantage is the nature of the two samples. The students were 17 or 18 in 1965. They could not vote and were much less developed politically than the adult population. Their parents are a better bet for our purposes, but they are still a long way from being a representative sample. For one thing, their age range is fairly restricted; three-quarters of them were between 40 and 54 in 1965. And since their children had stayed at school, they were themselves somewhat above the national average in education.[28] These disparities do not seem to be a significant source of bias.[29]

Data on the parental generation from the 1965–1973 and 1973–1982 panels are also summarized in table 5.2. The most striking thing about these figures is their resemblance to those from the 1972–1976 NES panel. Aggregate party switching was not notably greater in eight or nine years than in four. Twice as much time did not produce twice as much net change.[30] Indeed, the biggest difference between the data sets is the lower directional stability of Independent Republicans in the NES panel, from 1972 to 1976. Although not so one-sided in their partisan impact, the years from 1965 to 1973 were a time of extraordinary turmoil and governmental fail-

28. Jennings and Niemi, "The Persistence of Political Orientations: An Over-Time Analysis of Two Generations," *British Journal of Political Science* 8 (July 1978): 333–63.

29. Converse and Markus, "Plus ça change," 39.

30. The same finding emerges from comparisons of stability in two-year periods in the 1972–74–76 panel and from analysis of changes in the four-wave panel conducted as part of the 1980 National Election Study (the latter data can be found in Green and Palmquist, "Of Artifacts and Partisan Instability," 876–77). The fact that the aggregate change is not proportionate to the time available for change should inhibit anyone who thinks that a simple extrapolation of a two-year or four-year change will yield a useful measure of long-term party switching. Limiting the analysis to respondents who voted in both 1972 and 1976 produces slightly higher figures for directional stability, which is consistent with Green and Palmquist's measurement-error thesis. Looking only at voters does not alter our conclusions about the relative stability of leaders and outright partisans.

ure, full of challenges to established institutions, not least to the two parties. The modest differences in stability between leaners and outright partisans in the face of these pressures are further evidence that the former were far from neutral observers of the partisan struggle.

The younger generation, as one would expect, were considerably less constant in their party preferences, particularly during their first years after high school. Among those who had been Democrats in 1965, directional instability in 1973 ranged from 12 percent of strong identifiers to 18 percent of weak partisans and 24 percent of leaners. On the Republican side, all three identifier types were 26 or 27 percent directionally unstable. These data provide scant justification for judging younger leaners to be any less partisan than other members of their age group. Change in party identification in the next nine years was a good deal more modest, although still well above that of the parents; 7 percent of Strong Democrats, 14 percent of Weak Democrats, and 22 percent of Independent Democrats were directionally unstable. The eight-percentage-point gap between the latter two groups is just two points greater than in the 1973 reinterview. On the other hand, 16 percent of Weak Republicans were directionally unstable, compared to 13 percent of leaning Republicans and 8 percent of Strong Republicans. Once again, we find little in these comparisons to justify characterizing leaners as neutrals rather than partisans.

The earlier (1952–54–56) Michigan panel data on partisan stability have been used by W. Phillips Shively for an ingenious and widely cited defense of the conventional wisdom:

> If leaners are in fact partisans who call themselves independent, then they should act like other partisans when they decide to vote for the opposite party—they should generally retain the same party loyalty, while deviating from their expected vote. On the other hand, if their reported "leaning" is simply another statement of how they intend to vote, then a change in the party for which

they intend to vote should bring a corresponding change in the party to which they lean.[31]

Shively tested this idea by examining changes in partisan voting and party identification from 1956 to 1958 and from 1958 to 1960 among those respondents in the Michigan panel who voted in both elections in either pair of years. For example, did people who in 1956 called themselves Democrats and voted for a Democratic candidate and in 1958 voted Republican change their 1958 party identification to match their vote in that year? Since we assume party identification to be fairly stable, occasional defections in voting should not lead to a change in party identification. Thus those people who "follow" a change in vote with a change in party identification may be presumed to have a weak attachment to the party they claim to be closer to or with which they identify.

Comparing each of the three kinds of Democrats or Republicans, Shively found that strong and weak identifiers who defected to the other party tended not to change party, a finding consistent with the conventional understanding of party identification. About half the floating leaners, however, changed their identification in each pair of years, leading Shively to conclude that "based on still scant evidence, it appears that most 'leaners' should be considered independents who have used the follow-up question to indicate their intended vote."[32]

Several problems with Shively's analysis cast considerable doubt on his conclusion, however. One difficulty, which he concedes, is the very small number of cases: just twelve vote-changing leaners in 1956–1958 and nine in 1958–1960. With cell sizes this small, a change of two respondents yields a percentage change of over twenty points—hardly an adequate basis for conclusions as fundamental as whether leaners are really independent.

There is a reason for the small cell sizes that points up an-

31. W. Phillips Shively, "The Nature of Party Identification: A Review of Recent Developments," in *The Electorate Reconsidered*, ed. John C. Pierce and John L. Sullivan (Beverly Hills, Calif.: Sage, 1980), 234.

32. Ibid., 235.

other problem with this analysis. The cell sizes are so small because *most leaners did not change their vote* from one party to the other in either two-year period. Over 80 percent of partisan Independents voted for the same party in both years in each of the comparisons Shively examined. In fact, weak partisans were more likely than leaners to vote for different parties from one election to the next, a finding ignored by Shively that speaks directly to the point of whether leaners are really so different from outright partisans. Since the vast majority of leaners were constant party-line voters, one should not single out the handful of exceptions and use their behavior to characterize the entire group.

We have exploited the 1972–1976 panel to repeat Shively's analysis with two successive presidential elections rather than contrasting a presidential vote with one cast in an off-year election. There are slightly different ways of doing this, and Shively's article did not make clear which alternative he used. We chose to take all 1972 strong identifiers who voted in both 1972 and 1976 and divide them into two groups—those whose votes in the two years were cast for the same party's presidential candidate and those who voted for different parties. Then we compared the proportion of each group who changed parties from 1972 to 1976. The same procedure for weak partisans and leaners produces for each category of party identification a probability that people in that group would switch parties to "follow" their vote intention. These calculations are presented in table 5.3.

This quasi replication yields findings similar to Shively's about the tendency of the different groups of identifiers to "follow" their votes. The leaners who voted for different parties in the two years are indeed more likely to switch parties in accordance with their changed votes. The difference in changed identification between the constant and floating voters is greater for leaners (25 percent) than for outright partisans (10 and 12 percent). The number of cases is considerably larger than in Shively's analysis, but the same considerations nevertheless destroy one's faith that these calculations show leaners to be truly independent. For one thing, 70 percent of

Table 5.3

Change in Party Identification among Constant and Floating Voters, 1972–1976

	Probability of Change in Direction of Party Identification, 1972–1976			Percentage who voted for same party in 1972 and 1976
Identification in 1972	Respondents who voted for same party in 1972 and 1976[a]	Respondents who voted for different parties in 1972 and 1976[a]	Difference in probability of change in party	
Strong Partisans	.024 (165)	.143 (42)	.119	80
Weak Partisans	.030 (167)	.132 (53)	.102	76
Indep. Partisans	.069 (130)	.321 (56)	.252	70

[a]The number in parentheses is the number of cases from which we calculated the probability; that is, the total number of respondents of the given level of partisan intensity in the column.

all leaners voted for the same party's presidential candidate in both elections. This level of constancy, just a few percentage points below that of the outright partisans, is inconsistent with the notion that the leaners' partisanship only reflects short-term forces.[33]

Less than a third of the floating leaners switched parties, while Shively's theory predicts that all of them would. In other words, less than 10 percent of the leaners changed their vote between 1972 and 1976 and switched parties to reflect that changed vote choice. The behavior of the other 90 percent was consistent with conventional expectations of partisans: either voting the same way in consecutive elections or, if defecting, nevertheless retaining their party identification.

Much more comprehensive evidence on the leaners' relative susceptibility to short-term and interelection forces comes from John R. Petrocik's analysis of 151 surveys conducted for congressional, state, and local candidates from 1980 through 1983:

> Weakly identified Democrats appear slightly less responsive to short-term forces than leaning Democrats. . . . The

33. These calculations count as constant voters those people who voted for the same party's presidential candidate in the two elections, even if both votes were for the other party's candidate. That is, Strong Democrats who voted for Nixon in 1972 and Ford in 1976 are not distinguished from Strong Democrats who voted for McGovern and Carter. By the same token, Democrats in 1972 who voted for Nixon and then Carter are mixed in with Democrats who voted for McGovern and Ford. We repeated our analysis after removing those respondents whose 1972 vote did not match their 1972 party identification, defining "constant voters" as those who voted in both years for the candidate of the party with which they identified in 1972 and "floaters" as those who cast a party-line vote in 1972 and switched to the other party's candidate in 1976. This increased the proportion of constant voters by eight to 10 percentage points in each party-identification category. The difference in change in party-identification between floaters and constant voters was about the same for leaners and weak partisans but rose to 32 percent for the strong partisans.

We also categorized respondents who voted in both elections according to their 1976 party identification and then repeated the original calculation. The results were very similar to those in table 5.3, except that leaners and strong partisans had about the same proportion of constant voters.

difference is statistically insignificant. With Republicans, the difference between weak and leaning identifiers is the *reverse* of expectations and (fortunately) also statistically insignificant. . . . Moreover, independents are not consistently more responsive to interelection tides than other partisans.[34]

Attitudes toward the Two Parties

A dozen years ago, Philip Converse and Gregory B. Markus referred to "a rising proportion of the electorate refusing to report identification with either party, and insisting on being classed as independents, thereby swelling the neutral middle of the party identification continuum."[35] Although skeptical of the verb "insist," we think this passage does identify the heart of the controversy about Independents: Is "neutral" an appropriate label only for the Pure Independents, or does it accurately describe the attitudes toward the parties of all three varieties of Independents? As we have seen (p. 79) Warren Miller wrote that leaners should be considered true Independents partly on the basis of the weakness of "their psychological ties to the parties." He did not mention any actual measures of such affect. The Michigan questionnaires have numerous items about general and specific attitudes toward the two parties that we will analyze in this section to see if leaners are less favorable to their own party, friendlier or more hostile to the other party, or merely more indifferent than outright partisans.

One such measure is the "feeling thermometer" on which respondents are asked to indicate the warmth of their affect for various persons and groups: "Ratings between 50 degrees and 100 degrees mean that you feel favorable and warm toward the person. Ratings between 0 and 50 degrees mean that

34. John R. Petrocik, "An Expected Party Vote: New Data for an Old Concept," *American Journal of Political Science* 33 (February 1989): 55, emphasis in original.
35. Converse and Markus, "Plus ça change," 33.

you don't feel too favorable." "Democrats" and "Republicans" have been rated often on the thermometer, but "Democratic Party" and "Republican Party," which are probably more pertinent objects, have been rated only since 1978.[36]

We are not the first researchers to use the feeling thermometer as an aid to classification of leaners. Charles H. Franklin and John E. Jackson reported their findings as follows:

> There is a very strong, monotonic relationship between the seven-point [party-identification] scale and an alternative measure of partisanship, defined by the difference between Democratic and Republican feeling thermometer scores. . . . Thus the seven category traditional variable is consistent with the relative evaluation of each party, or with the unidimensional concept of partisanship.[37]

Unfortunately, Franklin and Jackson said no more about the relationships they observed, hence we have no way of reconciling their report with our very different findings, some of which may be found in table 5.4.

As expected, strong partisans on both sides are by far the most favorably inclined toward their own party, the coolest toward the other party, and generally least likely to give an indifferent 50 rating to either party. In 1988, Weak and Independent Democrats evaluated their party almost identically. They were not far apart in their views of the Republican party; more Weak Democrats gave it both negative and positive ratings. These two groups' mean thermometer readings for the Republican party were both 50. On the Republican side, differences between weak partisans and leaners were also modest (and short of statistical significance) when rating their own party. Thirty-four percent of the Independent Re-

---

36. Differences between leaners and weak partisans on thermometer ratings of "Democrats" and "Republicans" were tiny to nonexistent from 1972 through 1980.

37. Franklin and Jackson, "The Dynamics of Party Identification," 963.

Table 5.4

Feeling Thermometer Evaluations of the Democratic and Republican Parties, 1988

| | Democratic Party | | | | Republican Party | | | |
	Negative score	neutral	positive	mean	Negative score	neutral	positive	mean
Strong Democrats	1	4	95	84	53	24	23	39
Weak Democrats	4	15	81	71	35	25	40	50
Indep. Democrats	4	17	80	70	33	34	33	50
Pure Independents	18	44	38	54	16	43	41	56
Indep. Republicans	35	31	34	49	4	18	78	71
Weak Republicans	33	40	27	48	4	15	82	72
Strong Republicans	57	23	20	38	1	4	95	84

Note: Entries in each cell are the percentage of each type of identifier who rated each party as negative (0–49), neutral (50), or positive (51–100).

publicans rated the Democratic party favorably, as did 27 percent of Weak Republicans. On the other hand, just 31 percent of Republican leaners were neutral about the Democratic party, compared to 40 percent of Weak Republicans. The data for 1980 and 1984, not shown here, are equally cold comfort to scholars who believe that leaners and weak partisans differ in their evaluations of either party.[38]

Attitudes toward the two parties can also be measured by responses to the four "master code" questions: "Is there anything in particular that you like (don't like) about the Democratic (Republican) party?" We classified respondents by the combinations of positive and negative answers they gave. Most respondents fell into one of these six categories:

1. +Democrats, −Republicans
2. +Democrats, ±Republicans[39]
3. ±Democrats, −Republicans
4. −Democrats, ±Republicans
5. ±Democrats, +Republicans
6. −Democrats, +Republicans

A seventh category is respondents who gave the same type of answer (positive, negative, or balanced) about both parties. An eighth category accommodates respondents with nothing to say about either party. We define the first three categories as pro-Democratic, the next three as pro-Republican, and the seventh as balanced. Table 5.5 shows what percentage of each type of party identifier made pro-Democratic, balanced, and pro-Republican comments in 1988, as well as the percentage who had nothing to say about either party.

38. The data for 1980 may be found in our "Partisan Affinities," 171.

39. Most respondents whose comments were coded ± had both favorable and unfavorable things to say about the indicated party. This category also includes respondents who had nothing to say about one party and answered one or both questions about the other party. Readers should note, therefore, that a small number of respondents in the "favorable" categories in table 5.5 said nothing about the party we say they favor; they made only negative responses about the other party.

Table 5.5
Comments about the Two Parties, 1988

	Favorable to the Democratic Party	Balanced	Favorable to the Republican Party	Failed to Comment
Strong Democrats	77	4	4	15
Weak Democrats	54	8	12	26
Indep. Democrats	54	10	13	23
Pure Independents	20	7	13	61
Indep. Republicans	13	7	51	29
Weak Republicans	14	9	48	29
Strong Republicans	6	6	80	8

Note: See p. 99 for definitions of net favorable comments.

Sixty-one percent of Pure Independents had neither favorable nor unfavorable opinions of either party, more than twice as many no-comment responses as any other category. This is another illustration of the difference between the largely apathetic Pure Independents and the more opinionated leaners and outright partisans. Because so many of these genuine Independents have nothing to say, even the number with balanced comments is low: 7 percent in 1988, 13 percent in 1980, and 22 percent in 1976. The leaners, on the other hand, are no more reticient than weak identifiers, no more inclined to offer balanced observations about the two parties. Just as many of them have only favorable comments about their own party and as few have anything good to say about the opposition. The findings for other years are not always quite as gratifyingly neat as those for 1988, but they all show that the leaners are similar to

weak partisans in their positive affect for their own party, their
lack of enthusiasm for the other party, and their disinclination
to make balanced comments about either party.[40]

These master-code items provide the weakest evidence for
our thesis. Other measures of partisan affect show the leaners
to be as favorably disposed to their respective parties as the
weak partisans; in some cases, more so.

This conclusion emerges from analysis of responses to the
question about which party "would be most likely to get the
government to do a better job in dealing with [the most important problem the country faces, in the respondent's opinion]"
(see table 5.6). From year to year, the public's assessments of
the two parties change dramatically, as do the issues on which
they base those assessments. In 1980, the Democratic party was
held in much lower esteem than in previous years by all types
of identifiers. In 1982, the Republican party suffered this fate.

Over the years, leaners have been at least as likely as their
weak partisan counterparts to choose their own party. More
Independent Republicans than Weak Republicans selected
their own party in four of the last five presidential elections.
By the same token, they were less inclined to prefer the Democratic party in every year except 1972. In the same period
differences between Independent and Weak Democrats in preferences for the Democratic party were never greater than
three percentage points and since 1980 Weak Democrats have
been a bit more inclined to choose the Republican party to
solve the most important problem.

Except in 1972, Independent Democrats were somewhat
more likely than Weak Democrats—the gap ranges from
seven to eleven percentage points—to say there was no difference between the parties. This scrap of contrary evidence is
balanced by the opposite finding on the Republican side
where weak partisans tended to exceed leaners in denying
that either party would do a better job.

40. The counterpart of table 5.5 for 1976 and 1980 may be found
in our "Partisan Affinities," 173.

Table 5.6

Preferred Party to Deal with the Most Important Problem the Country Faces, 1972–1988

	Democratic Party					No Difference					Republican Party				
	1972	1976	1980	1984	1988	1972	1976	1980	1984	1988	1972	1976	1980	1984	1988
Strong Democrats	42	65	29	57	56	35	30	44	35	39	14	2	16	7	3
Weak Democrats	30	47	8	35	36	48	40	52	45	51	16	6	33	17	11
Indep. Democrats	33	45	7	35	34	42	47	63	52	58	17	3	26	12	7
Pure Independents	8	20	3	11	9	63	62	54	61	74	19	6	33	22	11
Indep. Republicans	12	11	2	5	7	37	61	24	41	61	43	25	71	53	29
Weak Republicans	9	14	3	6	7	44	55	28	50	57	39	19	64	43	34
Strong Republicans	4	8	0	2	3	34	42	13	19	37	56	47	84	79	59

Note: The rows for each year do not sum to 100 percent because we have excluded from this table, but not from the bases on which the percentages were calculated, those respondents who said they did not know which party would do a better job.

The pattern displayed in table 5.6 was also found in responses to questions asking which party handles inflation better and is better at keeping the country out of war. By the same token, leaners in each party gave appropriately partisan answers when expressing their feelings about whether "Democrats" and "Republicans" have "too much influence in American life and politics," "just about the right amount" or "too little influence."

Behavior versus Self-Image

Up to this point, we have measured leaners' partisanship by looking at their voting and attitudes toward the parties. In all these respects they resemble outright party identifiers.[41] These similarities fade when we look at another dimension—leaners' beliefs about their own behavior. A good starting point is the pattern of responses to this question, asked by the Michigan researchers between 1952 and 1980: "Have you always voted for the same party or have you voted for different parties for President?" Responses for eight presidential elections are tabulated in table 5.7.

Unlike the findings reported so far, these data support the conventional wisdom about Independents. Table 5.7 depicts the sort of smoothly monotonic relationship between party identification and voting loyalty that the traditional literature would lead us to expect. The great majority of strong partisans, about half the weak partisans, less than a third of partisan Independents, and about one-sixth of Pure Independents say they always vote for the same party's presidential candidate.

Viewed in isolation, these findings seem perfectly reasonable. If being an Independent implies lack of partisan ties, we would expect little year-to-year consistency in the way self-professed Independents vote. At every election they would

41. Their attitudes on issues also resemble those of outright partisans in each party, as we will show in chapter 7.

Table 5.7

Party Identification and Self-Reported Partisan Consistency in Past Presidential Voting, 1952–1980

| | *Percentage Who Say They Have Always Voted for the Same Party's Presidential Candidate* | | | | | | | | |
	1952	1956	1960	1964	1968	1972	1976	1980	Average[a]
Strong Democrats	89	84	78	84	77	72	61	69	79
Weak Democrats	75	62	48	57	52	40	44	43	54
Indep. Democrats	41	39	21	38	37	33	28	17	33
Pure Independents	16	16	16	12	15	19	22	17	17
Indep. Republicans	44	33	30	30	32	23	26	26	31
Weak Republicans	54	57	56	54	40	38	47	28	49
Strong Republicans	72	80	74	77	63	70	67	60	73

[a]Average of annual percentages.

make their decisions after pondering the issues, judging the candidates, and reflecting on the nature of the times. Table 5.7 suggests some partisan regularity on the part of the leaners, but at a much lower level than for weak partisans. Relationships similar to those shown in table 5.7 appear to be the principal evidence adduced in *The American Voter* in support of the fundamental proposition that the party identification scale measures a unitary dimension that proceeds in linear fashion from one pole to the other.[42] The same item was used by Nie

42. The only tables in *The American Voter* separating leaners and weak partisans on any measure of partisan affect or behavior are those about respondents' reported consistency in past presidential voting or past changes in party identification (pp. 125, 126, and 148). By the same token, the only such table in *Elections and the Political Order* (p. 218) is about claims to have voted for the same or different parties' presidential candidates.

and his associates to illustrate "the change in the strength of party ties from the 1950s to the beginning of the 1970s."[43] Some scholars believe that these retrospective reports on party loyalty are convincing evidence in favor of the conventional wisdom, even in the face of our findings about the actual voting choices of leaners.[44]

Table 5.7 becomes problematic when compared to other data on party loyalty. Although Strong and Weak Republicans are much more likely than their Democratic counterparts to vote for their party's presidential candidate in any given year, they are somewhat less likely to claim consistency in all past elections. Judging by their reported votes just after the election, Strong Republicans averaged 97 percent loyalty in the eight elections from 1952 through 1980. Yet during the same period only 73 percent of Strong Republicans said they always voted for the same party. These findings are difficult to reconcile, even if one assumes complete turnover in the ranks of disloyal Strong Republicans from one election to the next.[45] In order to take the data in table 5.7 as a measure of actual voting behavior, one would have to believe that at every level of party identification, Democrats are more loyal presidential voters than Republicans and that, in either party, the weak identifiers are more loyal than the leaners. This is the opposite of findings from data based on reports of voting in a single election.

The problem might be one of question validity: Which of the two questions is the better measure of party regularity? The item about voting in the immediately past election asks about a recent act; it does not severely test the respondent's

43. Norman H. Nie, Sidney Verba, and John R. Petrocik, *The Changing American Voter,* enlarged ed. (Cambridge: Harvard University Press, 1979), 54.

44. See, for example, Herbert M. Kritzer and Robert B. Eubank, "Presidential Coattails Revisited: Partisanship and Incumbency Effects," *American Journal of Political Science* 23 (August 1979): 617n–18n.

45. Another possibility is substantial turnover from one election to the next among people claiming to be Strong Republicans. The data in table 5.2 lead us to reject this alternative.

memory. This is not the case with the other question, which calls on respondents to remember behavior that may not be important to them and occurred at various times in the past. Doubts in general about such retrospective data are sustained by Richard A. Brody's analysis of panels in which the same respondents were reinterviewed at two-year intervals. Brody found that 71 percent of those people who identified with one party in 1956 and the other party in 1958 denied that they had ever switched parties. In the 1972–1974 panel, 58 percent of switchers reported that they had always identified with the same party.[46]

The 1972–1976 panel provides an opportunity to verify respondents' claims about their voting histories by comparing responses to these three items: (1) 1972 reports about past consistency, (2) the reported vote in 1972, and (3) 1976 reports about past consistency. Those respondents who said in 1972 that hitherto they had always voted for the same party and then voted for the other party's candidate in that year should without exception report four years later that they had voted for different parties. By the same token, people who claimed consistency and voted consistently in 1972 should all repeat their claim that they always voted for the same party. In fact, 30 percent of the consistent voters said in 1976 that they voted for different parties, and 27 percent of the actual inconsistents claimed that they had always been faithful to one party.

If such misreporting reflected nothing more than memory lapses, we would expect it to be evenly distributed across different categorics of partisans, modified only by variations in political involvement. But a question about always voting for the same party is probably not value-free. Some people prize a self-image as loyal partisans, and others might value the appearance of open-mindedness. The severity ("always")

46. Brody, "Stability and Change." Because of the obvious potential for motivated memory lapses when responding to the question about past changes in party identification, we dismiss *The American Voter* table (p. 148) that shows a monotonic relationship between this variable and the strength of party identification.

of the question compounds the problem, as does its location in the questionnaire. The item on past party regularity was asked shortly after the series of questions on party identification. Independents, having just declared this status, might want to describe their behavior consistently with their self-identification. Respondents unsure about their voting history might take the self-description as a cue: "I just called myself an Independent; therefore, I must vote for different parties."[47]

In short, there are reasons to suspect that some people who had been wholly faithful to one party might claim otherwise and that some inconsistent voters might insist on their loyalty. If this were true, we would expect that avowed partisans whom we discovered to be inconsistent voters in 1972 and 1976 would be more likely to make the false claim that they had always voted for the same party. This is what we found. Indeed, almost every one of these "concealed defectors" was a strong or weak partisan. Similarly, we found that both leaners and Pure Independents who voted consistently were much more likely than consistent partisans to deny that they always voted for one party.

The same pattern of systematic misreporting emerged when we examined the claims about past voting of only those respondents who in 1976 were old enough to have voted in just one previous presidential election. Along with the rest of the sample, they were asked in the preelection interview if they had voted in any past presidential elections for which they had been eligible to vote. Those who answered affirmatively were

47. In 1980, the question did not follow the standard set of items about party identification. Instead, it followed a new battery, tapping attitudes toward partisan commitment, the last item of which asked: "Do you ever think of yourself as a political independent, or not?" Leaners were by far the most likely to respond affirmatively, followed by Pure Independents, as the following figures for each type of identifier demonstrate: SD, 22; WD, 31; ID, 78; I, 64; IR, 79; WR, 33; SR, 27. It is no more surprising than for earlier years, therefore, that when asked to report on their partisan consistency as a sequel to affirming their independence, all three types of Independents in 1980 overwhelmingly reported not having voted for the same party over the years. We will discuss these 1980 questions in chapter 9.

asked whether they had always voted for the same party for President or for different parties. Their replies, tabulated against the seven-point party-identification scale, are presented in table 5.8.

The responses of these young voters differ in one respect from those of the entire sample: Republicans are more likely to profess party regularity. Otherwise, the distribution of responses resembles that for the whole sample. Strong identifiers are most likely to claim fidelity to one party, followed by weak identifiers, leaners, and Pure Independents. The catch, of course, is that *none* of these respondents could have voted in more than one prior presidential election. Thus it is difficult to see how any of them could have managed to avoid always voting for the same party. Yet only two-thirds of these young voters would acknowledge the irrefutable.

Given the findings in table 5.8, we believe that replies to the question about past voting measure self-image as well as

Table 5.8

Party Identification and Self-Reported Partisan Consistency of One-Time Voters, 1976

	Percentage of Respondents between the Ages of 22 and 28 Who Say They Have Always Voted for the Same Party's Presidential Candidate	Number of Cases[a]
Strong Democrats	66	27
Weak Democrats	56	76
Indep. Democrats	56	53
Pure Independents	50	49
Indep. Republicans	62	39
Weak Republicans	68	45
Strong Republicans	100	21

[a]Total number of young respondents in each category of party identification.

previous behavior. Considering this possibility, the authors of *The American Voter* wrote:

> In this discussion we assume that the concealed partisan is less likely to distort his voting record than his description of his party attachment; that is, we assume that what the undercover partisan values is chiefly the designation "Independent." To the extent this is untrue, the analysis of voting consistency by strength of party identification fails to enhance our understanding.[48]

With the benefit of many years of hindsight since these words were written, a better conclusion might be that the value the "undercover partisan" places on the designation Independent is sufficient to distort his memory.

The halo effect of being an Independent was anticipated by the Michigan researchers when they designed the questions about party identification. Warren Miller told one of us that the probe about leaning toward a party was based at least partly on the assumption that "being an Independent was a matter of civic virtue; for many people it was more socially acceptable" than being a Democrat or Republican. The probe, in other words, was designed to smoke out the Democrats and Republicans who were reluctant to come clean about their partisanship. The message of this book is that the goal was important and the method effective. If these simple propositions had been acted on consistently by the Michigan scholars and their successors and critics, this book would have been unnecessary.

The patterned misperceptions about past voting are useful data in several respects. On the negative side, they show why the voting-history item does not provide valid evidence for the conventional position on Independents. More generally, these findings are another nail in the coffin of the notion that

48. Campbell et al., *The American Voter*, 125n. The quoted passage refers to Pure Independents' answers to the question about past partisan consistency.

long-term retrospective data are a measure of reality.⁴⁹ Positively speaking, the findings help us think about the leaners' initial reluctance to acknowledge an affiliation consonant with their beliefs and behavior. Leaners resemble avowed identifiers in their voting choices and opinions about the two parties, but evidently are uncomfortable about being partisan. We interpret the data here and in chapter 4 as evidence that the leaners are party identifiers who hesitate to own up to their party ties despite an affinity scarcely less stable than that of Weak Republicans or Democrats. We suspect that their reluctance reflects at least in part the parties' low popular image. We view the second question in the NES party identification series as a probe to overcome that reluctance.

A completely different interpretation has been developed by Warren Miller, who argues "the utility of distinguishing between the overlapping concepts of partisanship and party identification."⁵⁰ The leaners "are demonstrably and overtly partisan," but they are not party identifiers.⁵¹ Miller's distinction is rooted in the different wording of the successive NES questions. Party identification is a durable self-identity that is appropriately measured by the first question's emphasis on the long view: "Generally speaking, do you usually think of yourself . . . ?" In contrast,

> the follow-on question, "Do you think of yourself as closer to the Republican or Democratic party?" does not attempt to elicit a qualified or limited sense of an "enduring engagement of partisan feelings with self-identity;" the question is asked only in the present tense, and it calls only for a cognitive assessment of current circum-

49. For more evidence on this point, see Richard G. Niemi, Richard S. Katz and David Newman, "Reconstructing Past Partisanship: The Failure of the Party Identification Recall Questions," *American Journal of Political Science* 24 (November 1980): 633–51.
    The flaw in the question about past voting history that is explained in this chapter led to its deletion from the NES questionnaire after 1980.
50. Miller, "Party Identification," 557.
51. Ibid., 558.

stance. The answers may indicate partisanship but they do not reflect a sense of party identification.[52]

Miller acknowledged that "the reasons for this strict interpretation of the meaning of party identification are more firmly grounded in theory than in data."[53] His distinction is not germane to our central purpose, which is to evaluate the assumptions about Independents that underlay the widespread discussions of dealignment described in chapter 1. Leaners exhibit none of the uncommitted traits attributed to Independents, hence trends in party identification since the late 1960s do not pose much of a threat to the American political system. From this perspective, it may not matter whether leaners are more properly considered party identifiers or only long-term fellow travelers.

In this chapter we have examined measures of partisan affinity other than vote choice to explore leaners' degree of neutrality and commitment. We conclude that the simplest explanation of their voting patterns is correct: They vote as they do because they are partisan, not neutral, about the two parties. Their partisanship is evident not only in their voting but in their choice of presidential primary elections, the stability of their party identifications, and their attitudes toward the two parties. In all these respects they resemble outright partisans and differ from Pure Independents, who profess no attachment to either party.

52. Ibid. The quoted passage is from Converse and Pierce, "Measuring Partisanship," 143.
53. Ibid.

6

Age, Education, and Dealignment

Our analysis up to this point has been largely static. What we found about 1988 or 1976 was equally true of the 1950s. Nothing changed very much, except that Pure Independents have even less civic virtue than they did a generation ago. Having made our case that leaners are essentially partisans who have nothing in common with the neutral Pure Independents, we turn now to describing the people most responsible for the growing numbers of Independents, a trend that we will call *dealignment* without prejudice to our argument about the leaners' partisanship.

We begin with the familiar and plausible proposition that independence, always more common among the young, was particularly appealing to those who reached voting age at the time of the Vietnam War. Was dealignment confined to the young, or did it also reflect abandonment of party identifications by some older Americans? A second question concerns the persistence of these independent identifications. Are the baby boomers becoming more partisan as they reach middle age? In other words, how general was dealignment, and how durable?

A third line of inquiry concerns the next generation, to whom Vietnam is history and Eugene McCarthy as remote as Joseph McCarthy. Are they as disinclined to identify with a party as their immediate predecessors, or do they have the more modest inclination to independence of those who first could vote before the death of President Kennedy?

This is not unexplored territory, but as we will see, differentiating leaners from Pure Independents makes possible a clearer description of trends in party identification in the past twenty-five years. The distinction is central to our analysis of education, the concluding topic of this chapter and the only other demographic variable helpful in understanding dealignment.

Age and Partisanship

Most scholars agree that the increase in Independents was a reaction to "shocks" that seemed sharpest in the decade that began in the mid-1960s: the failure of political institutions, including the two parties, to achieve satisfactory solutions to the country's most salient problems, the Vietnam War and racial conflict.[1] We will examine these interpretations directly in the next chapter. Here we concentrate on those citizens who seemed most susceptible to such shocks. Young people are widely believed to be more politically labile. Whether because they are more impressionable than their elders or because their political "anchors" are weaker, their reaction to dramatic political events is sharper and more durable than that of older citizens. It seems reasonable, then, to expect that young people would be found "at the cutting edge" of dealignment, that is, more inclined to be Independents.[2]

1. The most meticulous tracing of declining party identification is in Philip E. Converse, *The Dynamics of Party Support* (Beverly Hills, Calif.: Sage, 1976). He found the first marked drop in "mean party identification strength" occurred between 1964 and 1966; a second from 1971 through 1974. Converse did not measure an increase in Independents as such, however. His measure of party identification strength assigned a score of 3 to strong partisans, 2 to weak partisans, 1 to leaners, and 0 to Pure Independents.

2. M. Kent Jennings and Gregory B. Markus, "Partisan Orientations over the Long Haul: Results from the Three-Wave Political Socialization Panel Study," *American Political Science Review* 78 (December 1984): 1015.

The American Voter reported that even in the 1950s "young people, just entering the electorate, are more likely than any of the older age groups to call themselves Independents."[3] If Independents were progressively scarcer in older age groups, this might be a *life-cycle effect:* "party identifications strengthen with age."[4] The mechanism is thought not to be age as such; rather, age is a surrogate for the number of years an individual has been affiliated with a party. "Perhaps older citizens are more staunchly partisan because the repeated use of party labels to interpret and understand the political world through the years reinforces and strengthens one's partisan ties."[5] This interpretation "fits very well a more general thesis that group identification is a function of the proportion of a person's life he has been associated with the group."[6]

But any analysis of age and partisanship must account for conflicting interpretations of a relationship observed at a single point in time or over a brief period. If older respondents in the 1950s were likelier to be strong partisans, this might reflect not so much their place in the life cycle as the fact that their political perspectives were formed in an era when partisanship was more enthusiastic, widespread, and unquestioned. This is a *generation effect,* defined by Philip Converse as "a kind of early imprinting which . . . will always leave its characteristic mark" distinguishing the affected age cohort from other generations not so affected by the imprinting

3. Angus Campbell et al., *The American Voter* (New York: John Wiley and Sons, 1960), 161. This seemed to be the accepted position, but there were dissenters. See William H. Flanigan and Nancy H. Zingale, *Political Behavior of the American Electorate*, 4th ed. (Boston: Allyn and Bacon, 1979), 68.

4. Philip E. Converse, "The Concept of a Normal Vote," in Angus Campbell et al., *Elections and the Political Order* (New York: John Wiley and Sons, 1966), 18n.

5. Gregory B. Markus, "Dynamic Modeling of Cohort Change: The Case of Political Partisanship," *American Journal of Political Science* 27 (November 1983): 721.

6. Campbell et al., *The American Voter*, 163.

event or condition.[7] The defining characteristics of a generation effect are its limitation to an age-defined group and its
durability. A *period effect*, on the other hand, makes its mark
irrespective of age.

These formulations are somewhat problematic. No matter
how much one may believe in the susceptibility of the young,
it is difficult to imagine an event that would imprint one
generation for life without leaving a discernible mark on at
least some older people. Moreover, the effect of a gripping
event may linger for only a few years before the familiar life
cycle of strengthening partisanship resumes. If so, one must
be chary about judging any relationship to be evidence of a
generation effect. One might also discern an apparent period
effect limited to people beyond the first flush of youth, but
still short of middle age. As we will see, these caveats are
illustrated by evidence on the party identification of different
age groups from the 1960s through 1990.

We begin by examining the proportions of various age
groups in each of the three categories of independent identifi-

7. Converse, *The Dynamics of Party Support*, 74. For evidence of a
strong life–cycle effect in the "steady–state period" from 1952 to
1964, see *ibid.*, chap. 3. A number of studies have shown that for at
least a decade, beginning in the mid–1960s, party identification did
not strengthen as people grew older. See *ibid.;* Paul R. Abramson,
"Generational Change and the Decline of Party Identification in America: 1952–1974," *American Political Science Review* 70 (June 1976):
469–78, "Generational Replacement and Partisan Dealignment in
Britain and the United States," *British Journal of Political Science* 8
(July 1978), and "Developing Party Identification: A Further Examination of Life-Cycle, Generational, and Period Effects," *American Journal of Political Science* 23 (February 1979): 78–96. See also M. Kent
Jennings and Richard G. Niemi, "The Persistence of Political Orientations: An Over-Time Analysis of Two Generations," *British Journal of
Political Science* 8 (July 1978): 333–63; Norman H. Nie, Sidney Verba,
and John R. Petrocik, *The Changing American Voter*, enlarged ed. (Cambridge: Harvard University Press, 1979), 59–73.

These studies seldom distinguished among types of Independents.
The exceptions are Abramson and Converse, who used the coding
scheme described in note 1.

cation. These data for white respondents in each presidential election year from 1952 through 1988 are arrayed in table 6.1. The only one of these groups that is truly neutral between the parties—Pure Independents—had no special youth appeal in the 1950s. Not until 1964 were people under the age of 29 significantly more likely than the entire population to be Pure Independent. In 1968 a monotonic relationship between youth and pure independence emerged. Since then, the facts have matched the conventional wisdom that young people are especially disposed to independence and older people are not.

Much the same is true of Independent Democrats, although here reality matched the stereotype more readily. In 1952 everyone up to the age of 65 was equally likely to be an Independent Democrat. This category did not have any special youth appeal until 1956, when a consistent pattern began. Consistency is the last term one would apply to the relationship between youth and Independent Republicans. They are the only group to display a satisfying monotonic relationship in the 1950s, but this disappeared in 1960 and 1964. For a dozen years thereafter, the Independent Republican identity also seemed to appeal more to young people. In the 1980s, the only age group notably less attracted to this label was people 65 and over.

By 1968, the three varieties of independent identification were consistently most popular among people in their twenties. What is more, increasing proportions of youngsters reaching voting age were eschewing outright partisanship in favor of one or another sort of independent status.

Did this trend continue unabated through the 1970s and 1980s? Was the popularity of independence limited to the youngest set, or did older citizens come to share it? And what happened to the children of the sixties as they entered the second decade of their political maturity? Did they continue the disavowal of partisanship with which they entered political life? To answer these questions, we have made use of not only the simple cross-tabulations in table 6.1, but also analysis of eight age cohorts, which let us track party identification in each age group as it moved through the life cycle. In order to reduce sampling error by accumulating larger numbers of cases, we used eight-year cohorts, the youngest of which in 1960 were those respondents who had not been old enough to vote in 1952. We began with 1960 because it preceded the "shocks" to party identification described by Converse; 1968, of course, was the year of peak political tumult. Because of the ratification of the 26th Amendment in 1971, the group too young in 1976 to have voted eight years earlier had an age span of eleven years and our youngest cohort in 1984 had an upper age limit of 25 rather than 28. The availability of 1990 NES data shortly before this book went to press let us take one more look at the earlier cohorts and also at a new cohort of those aged 18 to 23. Our oldest cohort takes in everyone over 74 in 1990. The cohort data are presented in tables 6.2, 6.3, and 6.4.

All three varieties of independence increased, in a different pattern for each category. The proportion of Pure Independents grew most among young people, but we did find a limited amount of change among some older cohorts. There was no change among people who were at least 45 in 1960 (Cohort VII) and a four-precentage-point increase in Pure Independents from 1960 to 1968 in the next two cohorts. Thereafter, the only shift in these three cohorts was a gradual decline in their proportion of Pure Independents. The oldest group in which party identification declined sharply was Cohort IV, who came of age in the Eisenhower era and weathered the Johnson administration without gaining Pure Independents. But in 1976, when Cohort IV was 37 to 44, approaching middle age, its proportion of Pure Independents nearly doubled, to 19 percent. Just 8 percent of them were Pure Independents in 1984 and 11 percent in 1990, which is about where they were in 1960 and, for that matter, where everyone 45 and older was in 1960.

Among the prime candidates for disillusionment are those who reached political maturity in the 1960s, our Cohort III. Eighteen percent were Pure Independents in 1968, at least

Table 6.1 Age and Independent Identification, 1952–1990

	1952	1956	1960	1964	1968	1972	1976	1980	1984	1988	1990
Percentage of each age group who were Pure Independents											
21–28[a]	7	9	12	12	18	19	22	21	14	16	17
29–44	6	10	8	8	11	16	19	15	13	14	11
45–64	7	10	10	7	11	10	11	10	9	8	10
65+	6	7	10	6	7	7	9	8	8	8	6
Total	6	9	9	8	12	14	15	14	11	12	11
Percentage of each age group who were Independent Democrats											
21–28[a]	10	13	10	14	20	20	16	16	14	13	14
29–44	10	7	8	12	11	12	14	13	11	12	14
45–64	11	5	5	7	8	9	9	9	11	11	12
65+	7	3	3	4	5	6	8	10	7	7	7
Total	10	7	6	9	10	12	12	12	11	11	12
Percentage of each age group who were Independent Republicans											
21–28[a]	13	15	5	8	16	15	14	13	16	17	16
29–44	8	9	10	8	11	15	12	11	14	17	12
45–64	5	9	7	5	8	8	10	14	12	14	14
65+	7	4	2	5	5	6	7	6	11	10	9
Total	8	9	7	6	10	11	11	11	13	15	13

[a] Age 18–28 starting in 1972.

Table 6.2

Identification as Pure Independents by Eight-Year Cohorts, 1960–1990

	Percentage Who Were Pure Independents				
Cohort	1960	1968	1976	1984	1990
VII	Age 45+	Age 53+	Age 61+	Age 69+	Age 75+
	10	9	10	8	5
VI	Age 37–44	Age 45–52	Age 53–60	Age 61–68	Age 67–74
	8	12	11	9	7
V	Age 29–36	Age 37–44	Age 45–52	Age 53–60	Age 59–66
	8	12	11	9	7
IV	Age 21–28	Age 29–36	Age 37–44	Age 45–52	Age 51–58
	12	10	19	8	11
III		Age 21–28	Age 29–36	Age 37–44	Age 43–50
		18	19	13	10
II			Age 18–28	Age 26–36	Age 32–42
			22	13	11
I				Age 18–25	Age 24–31
				14	16
0					Age 18–23
					18
Total	9	12	15	11	11

half again as many as any other cohort in 1968. Cohort III were at the same place in 1976, when 19 percent of them eschewed any partisan affiliation. By 1990 this dropped to 10 percent, the norm for everyone but the youngest cohort thirty years earlier.

In 1976 the next generation, Cohort II, had spent their entire brief political lives in a time of disorder, discontent, scandal, and apparent bipartisan failure. Twenty-two percent of them were Pure Independents in 1976, the highest proportion for any cohort in any year. By 1990 this figure had dropped by half, to 11 percent, the same as the two preceding cohorts in 1990.

Next is Cohort I, those aged 18 to 25 in 1984, whose political perspectives were largely developed in the era after Vietnam and Watergate. Fourteen percent of them were Pure Independents in 1984. This is substantially lower than the reading for the first appearance of the two previous cohorts and is a statistically insignificant two percentage points higher than the proportion of Pure Independents in Cohort IV at its debut in 1960. Six years later Cohort I's share of Pure Independents rose from 14 to 16 percent. This may be nothing more than a blip, which we consider more plausible than taking it as a portent of another round of dealignment.

Finally there is the truncated Cohort 0, aged 18 to 23, who made their debut in 1990. Their relative youth may explain the 18 percent of this group who were Pure Independents.

In 1976 the three youngest cohorts had about the same one-fifth proportion of true partisan neutrals. In view of their age range, from 18 to 44, we consider this evidence of a limited period effect that stilled whatever relationship between age and increasing partisanship would usually be associated with movement through the life cycle. The three cohorts were also fairly similar eight years later, but at a sharply diminished level of independence. And by 1990 Cohorts II–IV had virtually the same proportions of Pure Independents as their counterpart age groups in 1960. In other words, after its suspension in the time of troubles, the familiar life cycle of strengthening partisan identification seems to have resumed in the (temporarily at least) more reassuring atmosphere of the Reagan administration. With the advantage of more time for hindsight, we can see that Paul Abramson was premature in concluding that the Vietnam-Watergate cohorts were fated to remain unusually withdrawn from partisan commitment:

> The overall weight of evidence for nearly a quarter of a century casts doubts on the life-cycle formulation. Instead, the overall results show considerable stability in partisan strength within cohorts as they age, suggesting that once formative socialization occurs persons tend to

retain their level of partisan strength as they move through the life cycle.[8]

Table 6.2 also displays the sharp differences betwen Cohorts II–IV and older citizens, those who were at least 29 in 1960 and therefore were well into their thirties when the time of troubles began. This generation gap can be seen most clearly in the 1976 column. In that year, one in five respondents under 45 were Pure Independents, double the proportion in the rest of the population. The proportion of Pure Independents among Cohorts V, VI, and VII was scarcely greater in 1976 than in 1960; differences for single cohorts observed in table 6.2 are below the level of statistical significance.

This conclusion is important enough to warrant repetition: There was no increase in partisan neutrality among Americans who had reached their forties before the nation was convulsed by Vietnam and racial conflict. The increase in Pure Independents was concentrated entirely among those who attained voting age in the 1960s and 1970s. In this conclusion we differ from Converse, who reported that strength of partisanship declined among the elderly and middle-aged as well as the young; and Warren Miller, who saw the disruptions and frustrations of the era creating "a period effect felt throughout the electorate."[9]

8. Abramson, "Developing Party Identification," 91. Later studies showing a revival of partisanship include Warren E. Miller and J. Merrill Shanks, "Policy Directions and Presidential Leadership: Alternative Interpretations of the 1980 Presidential Election," *British Journal of Political Science* 12 (July 1982): 308–9; and J. Merrill Shanks and Warren E. Miller, "Policy Direction and Performance Evaluation: Complementary Explanations of the Reagan Elections," *British Journal of Political Science* 20 (April 1990): 160.

9. Converse, *The Dynamics of Party Support*, 95–97. In 1968 Converse's three cohorts were aged 25–40, 41–56, and 57 and older. Miller, "The Electorate's View of the Parties," in *The Parties Respond*, ed. L. Sandy Maisel (Boulder, Colo.: Westview Press, 1990), 103. Miller found particularly significant contributions to dealignment by the young. His findings were based on the ratio of strong partisans to Pure Independents among four-year cohorts. Using a differ-

In contrast to Pure Independents, who continued to gain among young people in the 1970s, Democratic leaners reached their peak with this constituency in 1968. They lost ground by 1976 and continued to do so in the 1980s. In 1968, 20 percent of all whites under 29 (Cohort III) were Independent Democrats. Their proportion of this cohort fell to 14 percent in 1976. It fell again to 9 percent in 1984 and then rose to 14 percent in 1990. Cohort II, who arrived on the scene in 1976, were 16 percent Independent Democratic in that year, 13 percent in 1984, and 14 percent in 1990. The proportions were similar for Cohort I in 1984 and 1990 and Cohort O in 1990.

Democratic leaners became more numerous in the 1970s not because young people were more attracted to this identity, nor as a result of a broadly-based shift in the same direction. Instead, the increased proportion of Democratic leaners reflected the baby boom, which generated many more young citizens, more likely than older people to be Independent Democrats, but not more so in the 1970s than previously.

In all older cohorts (IV–VII) the increase in Independent Democrats from 1960 to 1976 was barely perceptible (and short of statistical significance); thereafter, there was a trace of movement in the other direction. Even more than with Pure Independents, increases in Independent Democratic identification were confined to the younger crowd.

Republican leaners resemble the other two types of Independents in one respect: their increase was greatest among younger cohorts. (In saying this we acknowledge the mild swings of Cohort VI as well as the sharp increase among Cohort V. After registering no change from 1960 to 1984, this latter group showed 17 percent Independent Republicans in 1990, when most of its members were in their sixties.) Cohort IV, who came of age in the Eisenhower administration, were just 5 percent Independent Republicans in 1960. This proportion doubled by

---

ent measure, Miller and Shanks reported a decline in partisanship among people who came of age as early as the 1940s; see "Policy Directions and Presidential Leadership," 308.

Table 6.3
Identification as Independent Democrats by Eight-Year Cohorts,
1960–1990

Cohort	Percentage Who Were Independent Democrats				
	1960	*1968*	*1976*	*1984*	*1990*
VII	*Age 45+*	*Age 53+*	*Age 61–68*	*Age 69+*	*Age 75+*
	5	5	7	6	4
VI	*Age 37–44*	*Age 45–52*	*Age 53–60*	*Age 61–68*	*Age 67–74*
	7	11	8	8	9
V	*Age 29–36*	*Age 37–44*	*Age 45–52*	*Age 53–60*	*Age 59–66*
	9	10	10	13	10
IV	*Age 21–28*	*Age 29–36*	*Age 37–44*	*Age 45–52*	*Age 51–58*
	10	12	13	9	11
III		*Age 21–28*	*Age 29–36*	*Age 37–44*	*Age 43–50*
		20	14	9	14
II			*Age 18–28*	*Age 26–36*	*Age 32–42*
			16	13	14
I				*Age 18–25*	*Age 24–31*
				13	14
0					*Age 18–23*
					15
Total	6	10	12	11	12

1968. The next cohort was 16 percent Republican leaners in 1968, and the three succeeding cohorts displayed about the same proportion when they made their debuts in 1976, 1984, and 1990.

In contrast to the other Independents, however, Republican leaners did not become scarcer as the 1970s passed into history; a decline from 1984 to 1990 was notable only in Cohorts VI and III. And as we just observed, when the next three cohorts arrived, they included as many Republican leaners as had their counterparts in past years.

How can we summarize this welter of findings? First, it is

Table 6.4

Identification as Independent Republicans by Eight-Year Cohorts,
1960–1990

	Percentage Who Were Independent Republicans				
Cohort	1960	1968	1976	1984	1990
VII	Age 45+	Age 53+	Age 61–68	Age 69+	Age 75+
	5	7	8	9	8
VI	Age 37–44	Age 45–52	Age 53–60	Age 61–68	Age 67–74
	10	7	9	13	8
V	Age 29–36	Age 37–44	Age 45–52	Age 53–60	Age 59–66
	10	12	11	9	17
IV	Age 21–28	Age 29–36	Age 37–44	Age 45–52	Age 51–58
	5	10	11	15	15
III		Age 21–28	Age 29–36	Age 37–44	Age 43–50
		16	13	15	11
II			Age 18–28	Age 26–36	Age 32–42
			14	14	12
I				Age 18–25	Age 24–31
				17	15
0					Age 18–23
					15
Total	7	10	11	13	13

clear that most of the increase in all three types of Independents came from those who entered the electorate from the middle 1960s through the 1970s. Fully 54 percent of Cohort III, aged 21 through 28 in 1968, were one or another type of Independent in that year. The same was true of 52 percent of Cohort II in 1976. In addition, Cohort IV became somewhat more independent. The older cohorts seemed scarcely affected. There was no increase in Independents among people who were at least 30 in 1960, and only a modest amount among those eligible to vote in that year. This finding is consistent with the proposition that longtime party identification builds resistance to short-term influences.

Second, it is equally clear that the cohorts largely responsible for the increase in Independents are becoming more explicitly partisan as they age. The familiar life-cycle effect of the steady-state period is reemerging. This trend is most complete with respect to Pure Independents, who in 1990 were a much smaller proportion of Cohorts II–IV than in 1968 or 1976.

Third, youngsters reaching voting age after 1976, Cohorts I and O, were less averse to identifying with a party than their counterparts in 1968 and 1976, but still were a bit more inclined to be Independents than were Cohort IV, those arriving on the scene in 1960. It is too early to tell how much of this difference reflects their lower age. These new additions to the electorate, socialized primarily in the era of Carter and Reagan, contribute importantly to maintaining the proportion of Independents at a higher level than in the steady-state period. The other dynamic factor here, of course, is the passing of the oldest, quite partisan, generation.[10]

What do these findings suggest about the future stability of the political system as the dealignment generation enters the age of maximum participation? The leaners are partisans. Thus what results from the distribution of partisan Independents as the population ages is not likely to have much to do with volatility, party responsibility, or similar issues. Wanting to *feel* independent, as leaners do, may well have psychological implications, but our concern, and the concern of most observers who discuss dealignment, is its political implications. In this regard, leaners do not differ substantially from outright partisan identifiers.

The shift toward Independents coincided with the entry into the electorate of the baby-boom generation and the enact-

---

10. For similar findings see Shanks and Miller, "Policy Direction and Performance Evaluation," 160.

ment of the 26th Amendment. Those people most inclined to be Independents became a much larger share of the voting-age population. The extent of this phenomenon can be seen in table 6.5, which shows the proportion of people under the age of 29 in each type of Independent and the white population as a whole. In 1960, young people accounted for just 12 percent of all whites and anywhere from 7 to 18 percent of the three kinds of Independents. In 1972, young people were 25 percent of the entire white sample and 32 to 42 percent of Independents. By 1990 these proportions had fallen to 21 percent of the sample, 25 percent of the leaners, and 32 percent of the Pure Independents.

These data provide further reason for thinking dealignment is fading. Young people are a smaller proportion of the electorate, relatively fewer of them are without partisan affinities, and more people in the older dealignment cohorts are moving from independence to partisan identification.

Education and Independence

As we noted in chapter 3, the earliest conception of the Independent was an ideal citizen, one who could "give close and constant attention to public affairs."[11] In large part, the rise of the Independent was "an opposition of intellectuals to political machines—and indeed, to parties as such."[12] The view that Independents were educated citizens continued through the first half of the twentieth century. This image, developed largely from observations by scholars and pundits, was affirmed by early survey research. In 1948 George Gallup reported that "the higher the voter is in educational scale, the

11. James Bryce, *Modern Democracies*, vol. 1 (New York: MacMillan, 1929), 47–48.
12. Howard Penniman, *The American Political Process* (Princeton, N.J.: Van Nostrand, 1962), 39.

more likely he is to be independent."[13] This conclusion was based on these figures:

Education	% Independent
grade school or less	23
high school	31
college graduate	39

The American Voter's oft-cited low assessment of Independents' civic virtue included no reference to their educational attainment, except this remark: "There is no significant relationship between strength of party identification and formal education."[14] A few years later Walter Dean Burnham's suggestion of a "new breed" of Independent was based on 1964 NES data showing that the "peak share of independents falls among high school graduates who have had some college education."[15] Burnham concluded that the "political parties are progressively losing their hold upon the electorate" and that the losses "have largely been concentrated among precisely those strata in the population most likely to act through and in the political system out of proportion to their numbers."[16]

Burnham was right to wonder about the apparent inconsistency between the 1964 data on Independents' education and the low levels of interest, knowledge, and participation attributed to them in *The American Voter*. But as we will see, his explanation of the anomaly and the implications he derived from it miss the mark. Nevertheless, well into the 1980s many journalists and scholars noted Independents' relatively high education, and some cited Burnham's new-breed hypothesis. Others thought that rising education contributed directly to a

13. Cited in Dayton David McKean, *Party and Pressure Politics* (Boston: Houghton Mifflin, 1949), 183.

14. Campbell et al., *The American Voter*, 479.

15. Walter Dean Burnham, *Critical Elections and the Mainsprings of American Politics* (New York: W. W. Norton, 1970), 123.

16. Ibid., 129, 130. For a more recent exposition of the new-versus-old thesis, see Frank Sorauf, *Party Politics in America*, 6th ed. (Boston: Little, Brown, 1984), 173–74.

Table 6.5

Proportion of Young People among Independents, 1952–1990

| | | | | | | *Percentage under the Age of 29* | | | | | |
	1952	1956	1960	1964	1968	1972	1976	1980	1984	1988	1990
Indep. Democrats	15	27	18	24	32	42	35	31	27	21	25
Pure Independents	17	15	15	24	26	35	35	35	25	26	32
Indep. Republicans	27	23	7	20	28	32	31	27	24	20	26
All White Respondents	16	14	12	16	16	25	25	24	20	18	21

putative loosening of party ties. These two passages exemplify many others:

The growth of Independents has come particularly in those persons with sufficient education to permit freedom from party cues.[17]

Better educated Americans are less apt to affiliate with parties, which they perceive as lacking substance, and are more apt to identify themselves as free-thinking independents.[18]

Implicit in these statements is a belief that education reduces the individual's need for the cognitive and perceptual road map provided by party identification.[19] This notion is not timebound; it should be as applicable to the 1950s as to the contemporary scene. One simple way to explore this proposition is to examine relationships between respondents' education and their identification as Independents. Table 6.6 displays the percentages of people at various levels of schooling who were Independent Democrats, Pure Independents, and Independent Republicans in five of the ten presidential-election years from 1952 through 1988. These five years exemplify all ten.

Table 6.6 shows that the more educated people are, the *lower* the probability they will be Pure Independents and the *higher* the probability they will be leaners. In 1952, 7 percent of the least educated were Pure Independents as opposed to only 2 percent of college graduates. In 1988, the figures were 15 percent as opposed to 6 percent. The only exceptions were in 1960 and 1964, when there was no relationship between education and identification as a Pure Independent. The story is just the opposite for leaners. In 1952, 20 and 13 percent of

17. Gerald M. Pomper, *Voter's Choice* (New York: Harper and Row, 1975), 34.

18. Richard T. Saeger, *American Government and Politics* (New York: Scott, Foresman, 1982), 228.

19. For a formal statement of this proposition, see W. Phillips Shively, "The Development of Party Identification among Adults: Exploration of a Functional Model," *American Political Science Review* 73 (December 1979): 1039–54.

Table 6.6
Education and Independent Identification, 1952–1988

Education	Percentage of Each Educational Category Who Were:		
	Indep. Dem.	*Pure Indep.*	*Indep. Rep.*
	1952		
0–11 years	10	7	6
12 years	8	7	10
Some college	8	4	10
College degree	20	2	13
Total population	10	6	8
	1964		
0–11 years	8	8	5
12 years	11	8	5
Some college	12	9	9
College degree	9	7	9
Total population	9	8	6
	1972		
0–11 years	8	14	7
12 years	12	16	12
Some college	14	12	15
College degree	15	10	15
Total population	12	14	11
	1980		
0–11 years	9	16	7
12 years	10	17	12
Some college	17	14	14
College degree	14	8	11
Total population	12	14	11

Table 6.6

(*continued*)

Education	Percentage of Each Educational Category Who Were:		
	Indep. Dem.	*Pure Indep.*	*Indep. Rep.*
		1988	
0–11 years	8	15	11
12 years	11	15	16
Some college	12	8	14
College degree	14	6	18
Total population	11	11	15

college graduates were Independent Democrats and Republicans, respectively, as opposed to 10 and 6 percent of the least educated. This greater tendency for the better educated to be leaners is found throughout the period, with occasional modest exceptions that do not disturb the generalization.

Following trends from 1952 to the 1970s and 1980s reveals a considerable increase in the proportion of uneducated people who were Pure Independents, no change in their inclination to be Independent Democrats, and a modest rise in the percentage who were Independent Republicans. The picture for the college educated is very different. In the 1970s there was a modest increase in their inclination to be Pure Independents that reversed in the next decade. By 1988 the proportion of college-educated people who were Pure Independents had reverted to the level of the early 1960s. On the other hand, educated people in 1988 were much more likely to be leaners than their counterparts in the late 1950s and early 1960s.

Because middle-aged and older Americans did not contribute to dealignment, we examine, in table 6.7, the relationships between education and independent identification of respondents under 29 and those aged 29 to 44. These more focused cross-tabulations elaborate our earlier findings and

Table 6.7

Independent Identification by Age and Education, 1972, 1980, and 1988

	Percentage of Each Educational Category Who Were:					
	Age 18–28			Age 29–44		
Education	Indep. Dem.	Pure Indep.	Indep. Rep.	Indep. Dem.	Pure Indep.	Indep. Rep.
	1972					
0–11 years	15	31	12	14	21	10
12 years	20	21	15	10	17	15
Some College	18	11	15	10	16	17
College degree	26	14	16	12	9	23
Total age group	20	19	15	12	16	15
	1980					
0–11 years	3	45	16	11	23	10
12 years	11	23	15	11	23	11
Some College	25	12	11	18	6	13
College degree	15	17	12	13	8	10
Total age group	16	21	13	13	15	11
	1988					
0–11 years	8	30	20	11	27	11
12 years	14	17	21	9	18	14
Some College	12	15	12	12	8	15
College degree	13	4	11	15	8	24
Total age group	13	16	17	12	14	17

demonstrate the striking divergences in the party identification of young people according to their educational attainment. It is clear that the appeal of genuine partisan neutrality
is inversely related to education. Pure Independents are most
common at the lower end of the educational distribution and
become progressively scarcer as the level of schooling in-

Table 6.8

Leaners and Pure Independents among the Most- and Least-Educated
People under 29, 1968–1988

	1968	1972	1976	1980	1984	1988
Percentage of those who did not graduate from high school who were:						
Pure Independents	41	31	25	45	25	30
Partisan Independents	23	27	23	19	30	28
Percentage of college graduates who were:						
Pure Independents	13	14	14	17	5	4
Partisan Independents	44	42	34	27	36	24

creases. On the other hand, Pure Independents are scarce among younger college graduates, who are inclined toward partisan independence.

These differences are most pronounced among young citizens at the opposite ends of the educational spectrum—college graduates and those who had not graduated from high school. This can be seen more easily in table 6.8 where we show the proportion of the least- and most-educated respondents under the age of 29 who were leaners and Pure Independents in each election year from 1968 to 1988. In 1968, fully 41 percent of the unschooled young were Pure Independents. The proportion subsequently fell to a little over a quarter, except in 1980 when 45 percent of all the uneducated young disavowed any partisan identity. In contrast, just 13 percent of young college graduates were Pure Independents in 1968. The proportion scarcely rose above this level for the next three elections and then dropped sharply in 1984 and 1988 to 5 and 4 percent.

The popularity of partisan independence has had a very

different pattern; 23 percent of the less educated were leaners in 1968, and 27 percent in 1972. This number scarcely changed thereafter. On the other hand, 44 percent of young college graduates were leaners in 1968 and 42 percent were in 1972. Thereafter, the number fell unevenly to just 24 percent in 1988. In that year, only 28 percent of the best-educated younger generation were any sort of Independent, in striking contrast to 1968 when this was true of 57 percent.

We now can understand Pure Independents' declining voting rate. A growing proportion of them are near the bottom on the two demographic variables that are strongly related to turnout—age and education.[20] Controlling for these variables smoothes out the turnout variation among the seven party-identifier categories but does not erase Pure Independents' last-place ranking or leaners' relative civic virtue.

Other demographic differences between the varieties of Independents and outright partisans are without theoretical meaning or are a function of the age and education relationships we have just examined.[21] In any event, these differences seldom are very substantial. As we would expect, poorer people are more likely to be Pure Independent, while the better-off in particular favor the Independent Republicans. None of the findings reported in this chapter is consequentially altered if all Southern respondents are removed from consideration.

Summary

We have found one thing that all three types of Independents have in common: All are most appealing to young people. This was most clearly the case from 1968 through 1976 when over half of all whites under the age of 29 were Independents. The effect of this development was enhanced by the baby boom and the 26th Amendment, which were responsible for

20. Raymond E. Wolfinger and Steven J. Rosenstone, *Who Votes?* (New Haven: Yale University Press, 1980), chaps. 2, 3.
21. For example, Pure Independents are most likely to be found among "nontraditional" religious believers such as Mormons, Quakers, and Jehovah's Witnesses.

an unusually large addition to the electorate in the period when young people were most drawn to independence. By 1990 Cohorts II and III had scarcely more Pure Independents than their counterparts in 1960. One might say that the life cycle of strengthening party identification resumed after its apparent suspension. If this trend continues, the dealignment cohorts increasingly will resemble older citizens. This convergence argues against diagnosing their youthful independence as a generation effect in the sense of a permanent imprinting resulting from a profoundly moving event. New arrivals in the electorate since 1976 are neither as independent as their immediate predecessors nor as given to explicit partisanship as the oldest cohorts. At the other end of the age spectrum, Americans born before 1930 made no contribution to dealignment and those who reached voting age in the 1950s became notably more independent only by 1976. This in-between cohort then reverted to its pre-Vietnam pattern, except for an unusually large proportion of Republican leaners.

Our major theme about the fundamental differences between leaners and Pure Independents was revisited when we examined relationships between education and party identification. Better educated people were more likely to be leaners, less likely to be Pure Independents. These relationships strengthened over the years and among young people.

The tendency for most highly educated Independents to be leaners is not helpful to the notion that the high educational attainment of Independents suggests a considered and deliberate rejection of the American two-party system. As we saw, particularly in chapter 5, leaners show no signs of rising above the parties. And as we have seen and will see again, the only group that seems without affective ties to the parties, the only one without inhibitions about flocking to a new party, is the largely apathetic Pure Independents. These correspond to Burnham's "old independents" with respect to interest and participation, and in other respects seem unlikely to provide a constituency for either realignment or a new party. As we will see in the next chapter, Pure Independents are the least ideological and issue-oriented of the seven identifier types.

7

Issues and Dealignment

Many of the political issues that attracted public attention in the late 1960s and early 1970s were wholly new or had not previously been of more than peripheral interest: Vietnam, urban unrest, busing, women's equality, drug use, and conservation of natural resources. The new issues quickly came to be discussed in the same old ideological terms. Opposition to the war, support for the women's movement, a relaxed view of drug use and abortion, and a protective attitude toward the environment were all considered liberal views. This made things easy for editorial writers but did nothing to solve the problems of politicians who were trying to develop positions on the new issues that would be consistent with existing responsibilities, coalitions, and ideological inclinations. The war was a special difficulty in this respect while Lyndon Johnson was in the White House because the Democratic party could not easily become the vehicle of the peace movement as long as its president was the architect of the war. This source of dissonance faded as Richard Nixon assumed Johnson's role as a war president.[1]

1. Republicans were more hostile to the war when Johnson was president, but by the time Nixon had been in office for eight months,

Other considerations constrained an easy merging of the new issues and existing partisan alignments. Simply put, people who were liberal on the new issues often were conservative on the economic concerns that had dominated political controversy. Economic liberalism is most appealing to people who work with their hands and least popular among executives and professionals. But interest in the new issues and liberal attitudes on them were both greatest among educated people, who were likely to have white-collar jobs. This strain was most evident in the Democratic party. Millions of its traditional followers, particularly blue-collar workers and rural Southerners, had neither interest in nor sympathy for gun control, abortion, women's liberation, campus demonstrations, black militancy, hippiedom, or similar issues and symbols. At the same time, these activities and the issues they represented were powerfully appealing to millions of young people. If the Democratic presidential nomination seemed a victory for the old politics, as in 1968, then the Democrats seemingly risked losing the support of the new-politics adherents. And when the nomination brought the new-politics faction into control, as in 1972, the loyalty of traditional Democrats was jeopardized. Although similar conflicts were never as conspicuous in Republican ranks, the leadership of Richard Nixon did not suggest receptivity to the new politics.

This period of new issues coincided with the trend toward more Independents, a coincidence that led many political scientists to argue that the old party coalitions were being eroded by the concerns of a new generation of voters. Their argument was vividly summed up by Morris P. Fiorina:

> The 1960s witnessed the rise of issues that impinged on the everyday lives of American citizens. These issues, moreover, cut across existing party alignments. A Demo-

---

Democrats had become the greater opponents. "Johnson's war" became "Nixon's war." See John E. Mueller, *War, Presidents, and Public Opinion* (New York: John Wiley and Sons, 1973), 117.

cratic president sent the sons of the working class to die in a far-away war. The urban strongholds of the Democratic party degenerated into a battleground where race fought race and criminals plundered society. Meanwhile, the adolescent children of the upper middle class gleefully seized the opportunity to overthrow moral and behavioral standards which their parents evaded but generally accepted. Facing such conditions a party identification based on the Great Depression seemed increasingly removed from the politics of the 1960s. Some disillusioned party identifiers moved into the ranks of the independents. And large numbers of the maturing baby boom, finding little that was relevant to their concerns in the existing party system, did likewise.[2]

The numerous political scientists who made these arguments seldom went into detail about how the new issues led to dealignment.[3] These topics will occupy us in this chapter. Our search for issues that might plausibly be considered causes of dealignment has been largely fruitless.

Vietnam and Other Issues

There is no scarcity of confident assertions that the war in Southeast Asia started Americans on the road to dealign-

2. Morris P. Fiorina, *Congress: Keystone of the Washington Establishment* (New Haven: Yale University Press, 1977), 24.
3. Even in the 1950s people who were liberal on some issues were often conservative on others, and attitudes on issues generally did not coincide very well with party identification. On the first point, see V. O. Key, Jr., *Public Opinion and American Democracy* (New York: Alfred A. Knopf, 1960), 153–81. On the second point, see Herbert McClosky, Paul J. Hoffman, and Rosemary O'Hara, "Issue Conflict and Consensus among Party Leaders and Followers," *American Political Science Review* 54 (June 1960): 406–27. As early as 1972, evidence was available that there was not much consistency in attitudes even on such prototypical "new politics" issues as drugs and political demonstrations. See Teresa E. Levitin and Warren E. Miller, "The New Politics and Partisan Realignment," paper delivered at the 1972 annual meeting of the American Political Science Association.

ment.[4] The truth of this proposition was evidently considered so clear that there was no need to be more specific about the kinds of people who were thought to be most affected by the war, except to say that they were disproportionately young.[5] But what sorts of young people? Doves shocked at the waste of blood and treasure, hawks frustrated by Lyndon Johnson's slow escalation and restrictions on the military, people of either persuasion who thought Vietnam unimportant to American interests or judged our policy there a failure? Or all of the above?

An answer of sorts may be implicit in the only data cited by any of the scholars named in note 4: Gregory B. Markus's analysis of interviews in 1965 and again in 1973 with samples of high school seniors (in 1965) and their parents. On the basis of three questions about Vietnam and the military asked in 1973, Markus divided the parent and the offspring samples into three groups of equal size: "hawk," "middle," and "dove." Among the parents, the proportion of Independents (broadly defined) did not change from 1965 to 1973 in the hawk and middle groups, while among the doves it rose from 26 to 35 percent. Among the offspring, the proportion of Independents grew by six percentage points among the hawks, eight points in the middle group, and 17 points among the doves.[6] In view of the disparate partisan affinities and levels of civic virtue among the three kinds of Independents, all of whom were combined in Markus's analy-

4. For example, see Walter Dean Burnham, "The End of American Party Politics," *Transaction* 7 (December 1969): 12; Philip E. Converse, *The Dynamics of Party Support* (Beverly Hills, Calif.: Sage, 1976), 106; M. Kent Jennings and Gregory B. Markus, "Partisan Orientations over the Long Haul: Results from the Three-Wave Political Socialization Panel Study," *American Political Science Review* 78 (December 1984): 1015; Norman H. Nie, Sidney Verba, and John R. Petrocik, *The Changing American Voter*, enlarged ed. (Cambridge: Harvard University Press, 1979), 350.

5. In fact, young people were more, not less, supportive of the war. See Mueller, *War, Presidents*, 139.

6. Gregory B. Markus, "The Political Environment and the Dynamics of Public Attitudes," *American Journal of Political Science* 23 (May 1979): 346.

sis, this is a pretty flimsy case for pinning the blame for dealignment on the war in Southeast Asia. It is, however, the closest thing to a detailed empirical analysis that we know of.

For the most part, the Michigan surveys from 1966 through 1972 show weak to nonexistent relationships between any variety of independence and believing it was either right or wrong to go into Vietnam in the first place, to favor either a greater military effort or complete withdrawal, or saying that the war was an important influence on one's 1968 presidential vote. These findings may reflect the two parties' ambiguous policy stands during much of the war. In 1968, when public concern about Vietnam was near its peak, neither major party candidate offered clear proposals about what to do. Many voters saw little difference between them: "Members of the public were entirely justified in seeing Nixon and Humphrey standing close together near the center of the Vietnam policy scale, far from extremes of immediate withdrawal or escalation for complete military victory."[7] What is more, voters who did think the candidates had different positions were often engaged in wishful thinking:

> Those who saw a big difference between Humphrey and Nixon—a difference in either direction—were generally perceiving each candidate as standing wherever they wanted him to stand. They projected their own opinions onto their favored candidate. Among Republicans, who mostly favored Nixon, extreme hawks thought that Nixon was an extreme hawk; extreme doves thought he was an extreme dove; and those in the middle thought that Nixon stood in the middle! . . . Similarly, among Democrats . . .[8]

One might think that the picture had cleared four years later when George McGovern secured the Democratic presidential nomination on the strength of his uncompromising opposition

7. Benjamin I. Page and Richard A. Brody, "Policy Voting and the Electoral Process: The Vietnam War Issue," *American Political Science Review* 66 (September 1972): 985.
8. Ibid., 987.

to the war, but the public in 1972 did not completely agree. Less than two-thirds of those who supported withdrawal from Vietnam thought that McGovern agreed with them.

Although motivated misperception may have affected the Vietnam War's impact on both voting and party identification, it would be wrong to conclude that the issue was inconsequential in the 1968 election.[9] By the same token, both hawks and doves might have been moved to forsake outright partisan affiliation because neither major party's candidate provided a voice for their beliefs. Our analysis of the possibly dealigning effect of the war will, therefore, not attempt to relate policy preferences to party identification, but will concentrate instead on citizens' assessments of governmental performance and the positions they attributed to candidates and parties.

Assuming that the dealigning effect of an issue would be greater among people who considered the issue important, we begin our analysis by examining the magnitude and distribution of concern about Vietnam from 1966 through 1972. We chose to start with 1966 for two reasons: Converse found that the first shock to partisanship occurred in 1965;[10] and to our surprise, more respondents said Vietnam was the most important problem "the government in Washington should try to take care of" in 1966 than in any of the following election years.[11]

9. Hawks and doves alike who were dissatisfied with Lyndon Johnson's conduct of the war were more likely to vote against Humphrey than were those who approved Johnson's performance. See Richard W. Boyd, "Popular Control of Public Policy: A Normal Vote Analysis of the 1968 Election," *American Political Science Review* 66 (June 1972): 429–49.

10. Converse, *The Dynamics of Party Support*, 69–72. We found that the proportion of Independent Democrats remained stable from 1964 to 1966, that of Republican leaners rose from 6 to 7 percent of the white population in this two-year period, and that of Pure Independents rose from 8 percent in 1964 to 12 percent in 1966.

11. Our analysis of responses to the question about the most important problem includes only those for whom Vietnam (or the other concerns mentioned later) was the first issue mentioned or the issue the respondent concluded was most important.

Table 7.1

Vietnam and Urban Unrest as the Country's Most Important Problem,
by Age, 1966–1972

	Age				All White Respondents
	18–28	*29–44*	*45–64*	*65+*	
1966					
Vietnam	57%	48%	45%	41%	47%
Urban unrest	4	5	6	8	5
1968					
Vietnam	44	43	41	47	43
Urban unrest	16	18	19	14	17
1970					
Vietnam	37	34	26	20	29
Urban unrest	14	17	22	25	19
1972					
Vietnam	31	26	20	20	27
Urban unrest	3	5	8	6	5

Note: The number in each cell is the percentage of all respondents in the indicated category who mentioned Vietnam or urban unrest as the country's most important problem. In the first three years, the question was "What do you personally feel are the most important problems which the government in Washington should try to take care of?" In 1972, the wording was "What do you think are the most important problems facing this country?"

Table 7.1 shows that the level of concern about Vietnam declined from its 1966 peak of 47 percent to 43 percent in the troubled 1968 election, then dwindled to 29 and 27 percent two and four years later. A similar decline is found for each of the four age groups, except for a discordant note in 1968 for those over 64. Reading from left to right across the table for any year, one sees that worry about Vietnam was greatest among the young and declined with age (once again with the exception of the oldsters in 1968).

This is a promising start, but no more than that. The next

step is to see if respondents for whom Vietnam was important, particularly young respondents, were more likely to be
one or another variety of Independent. There was no such
relationship in the entire sample, but we did see one for respondents under 29. Twenty-one percent of those under 29
who considered Vietnam the most important problem were
Pure Independents, compared to just 7 percent of the remainder of their age group. Of the youngsters who cared about
Vietnam and thought neither party would do what they
wanted on that issue, 24 percent were Pure Independents.
Young respondents who thought the United States should
have stayed out of Vietnam were half again as likely (19 as
opposed to 12 percent) to be Pure Independents. There were
no consequential differences in other age groups. We found no
meaningful patterns involving leaners of either persuasion.
The only exception is this finding: Respondents under 45 who
advocated a "stronger stand" in Vietnam were somewhat
more likely to be Independent Republicans. This tendency
was a bit stronger among those who said they were paying "a
good deal of attention . . . to what is going on in Vietnam."

This promising start exhausts the items available in 1966.
But the trail peters out thereafter. Neither repetitions of the
analyses we have just described nor the others possible with
the plethora of Vietnam questions available in 1968 and later
years provides much reason to think that, whatever its other
effects on American electoral politics, this issue had much to
do with loosening identification with either major party.

In 1968, 1970, and 1972, those people who thought that
Vietnam was the most important issue facing the country
were no more likely than the rest of the sample to be Pure
Independents or leaners in either direction. Confining the
analysis to younger people did not change the picture.

We also identified those who seemed particularly disturbed
about Vietnam in 1968 with the question asking respondents if
there was "anything in particular that you don't like about the
Democratic party." We were surprised to learn that just eighty-
five whites brought up Vietnam. These people, to whom the

issue was very salient, had the same proportion of Republican leaners and a smaller share of Pure Independents than the entire sample. Nineteen percent were Independent Democrats, but any thought that this may be a useful clue should be cooled by noting that this is a mere sixteen respondents. People so concerned about Vietnam were not concentrated in any age group. A trivial number of respondents mentioned Vietnam in 1972 when answering this question or its counterpart about the Republican party.[12]

The war in Vietnam was a failure first by a Democratic president then by a Republican one. Both before and after the White House changed hands, the opposition party was at least partially inhibited from offering a thoroughgoing alternative policy. This is the background to the assumption that many Americans abandoned or never developed party identification because neither party's position satisfied them. Many committed doves could have been moved to forsake their party identification because of both parties' failures to recognize their feelings in 1968, and by McGovern's fuzzy image in 1972. By the same token, fervent hawks who had hoped to find a major party spokesman might have been deeply affronted by the outright opposition to escalation in Vietnam by Humphrey, Nixon, and McGovern.

Therefore we looked for concentrations of Independents among those who professed to find no difference between the parties in satisfactory performance on Vietnam when they considered it the most important problem.[13] Our search was rewarded in 1968, when 17 percent of those who saw no difference between the parties were Pure Independents. There was

12. Just eleven respondents said that Vietnam was a reason to dislike the Republican party.

13. When asked in 1970 "Which party do you think is more likely to do what you want?" concerning Vietnam, 61 percent of whites said there would be no difference between them. There was not much variation by age in this response. Respondents who saw the parties alike on this question were much more likely to be Pure Independents, especially among the young. There were no such relationships for leaners.

no greater relation among the young, however, and no tendency for such people to be leaners. We could not duplicate even this pallid finding in 1970 or 1972. We had no greater success when we limited our analysis to respondents who said they were "extremely concerned" about the problem they considered most important.

Another approach was to examine the gap between respondents' attitudes about Vietnam policy and those they attributed to the two parties to see if those furthest from a party were more likely to be some type of Independent. Unfortunately, the 1968 Michigan survey did not ask respondents to estimate the parties' stands, but it did ask about the presidential candidates' positions. We will use replies to this question as a surrogate for estimates of the parties' positions in 1968 and then use the more direct measure in 1970 and 1972. Here are the key sections of the question:

> Some people think we should do everything necessary to win a complete military victory, no matter what results. Some people think we should withdraw completely from Vietnam right now, no matter what results. And, of course, other people have opinions somewhere between. . . . Suppose the people who support an immediate withdrawal are at one end of this scale . . . at point number 1. And suppose the people who support a complete victory are at the other end of the scale at point number 7.

We divided the 1968 sample into four groups: those who put themselves and Humphrey at the same place on the seven-point scale, and those who were one point, two points, and three or more points away. We did the same for Nixon. In 1970 and 1972 we repeated this procedure for the parties rather than the presidential candidates. In all six analyses, as expected, there was a tendency for those close to Humphrey or the Democratic party to include more Democrats. By the same token, respondents closer to Nixon or the Republican party were more likely to be Republicans. In 1968 and 1970 we found some tendency for the proportion of Pure Independents to increase as the disparity grew between respondents and each of the four reference points (Humphrey, Nixon, Democratic party, Republican party). Sometimes these relationships were greater among the two younger age groups; for example, in 1968, among those 29–44, 18 percent of those furthest from Nixon were Pure Independents, compared to 9 percent of those who saw themselves in agreement with Nixon. There were no consistent tendencies for leaners on either side, in any age group. And in 1972 even the modest relationships observed in earlier years were absent. Finally, we looked at those respondents who were far away from *both* Humphrey and Nixon or from both parties. Here again, we found little connection between Vietnam and dealignment.[14]

Having spent so much space describing our search for a link between Vietnam and dealignment, we can quickly tell the story about urban unrest, another new, dramatic, protracted and unsettling issue of the period.[15] From 1968 through 1972, we found no significant relationships between any breed of Independent and concern about urban unrest, preferences for ways to deal with the problem, or perceived differences between one's position and that attributed to Humphrey or Nixon in 1968 or to either party in 1970 or 1972. The same was true of busing in 1972. The nearest approach to a pattern was a modest tendency for Pure Independents to be more common

14. Thinking that the war at home might have some connection with dealignment, we looked at the party identifications of respondents according to their feeling thermometer ratings of "Vietnam War protesters." The protesters, not very popular with anyone, were most warmly regarded by the youngest age group, 21 percent of whom had a favorable opinion of them, roughly half again as many as the older respondents. Admirers of protesters were more likely to be Democrats and had no tendency to be any variety of Independent.

15. Dissatisfaction with the Johnson administration's handling of urban unrest, while not as damaging as unhappiness about Vietnam, nevertheless contributed significantly to Humphrey's defeat in 1968. See Philip E. Converse et al., "Continuity and Change in American Politics: Parties and Issues in the 1968 Election," *American Political Science Review* 63 (December 1969): 1083–1105.

among those in disagreement with the Democratic party and in agreement with the Republican party. By 1976, even this hint of a relationship had disappeared.

Then there is Watergate, often linked with Vietnam and urban unrest as one of the seminal traumas of the era, and nominated by some scholars as a contributor to dealignment. For example, Philip Converse wrote, "I am not uncomfortable in presuming that the sequence of events known as Watergate had a prime role in the post-1972 phase of the second shock."[16] Traumatic as Watergate may have been, it differed from the other two issues in several important respects. For one thing, it did not go on for long; scarcely two years intervened between the arrest of the would-be telephone tappers and President Nixon's departure from the White House. That resignation brought an end to the crisis as a major news item, although trials and book publications continued for years. And of course Watergate was not a failure of both parties to deal with a problem.

Perhaps because the issue was not very salient during the 1972 campaign and was resolved in the summer of 1974, the NES provides few traces of popular concern with it. Just 20 respondents interviewed after the 1974 election said that Watergate was "the single most important problem the country faces." Another 60 people thought that insufficient personal ethics in government was the leading national problem. Leaners were somewhat scarcer among these 80 respondents than in the rest of the sample. Pure Independents were more common in this group, but nevertheless represent only 20 people. We conclude that Watergate was irrelevant to dealignment.

Party Differences

We proceed to examine the possibility that the increase in Independents reflected growing doubts that the major parties

16. Converse, *The Dynamics of Party Support*, 105.

Table 7.2
*Beliefs about Party Differences and Party Identification, 1972
and 1988*

| | Are There Important Differences between Democrats and Republicans? | | | | | |
| | 1972 | | | 1988 | | |
	Yes	No	Don't know	Yes	No	Don't know
Strong Democrats	12%	10%	8%	17%	11%	13%
Weak Democrats	26	26	40	16	21	16
Indep. Democrats	12	10	8	12	10	10
Pure Independents	8	15	15	5	20	20
Indep. Republicans	11	15	5	14	15	15
Weak Republicans	14	17	15	15	16	16
Strong Republicans	17	7	10	21	8	11
	100%	100%	101%	100%	101%	101%
(N) =	(441)	(451)	(93)	(924)	(528)	(82)

differed meaningfully, irrespective of any specific issue. The Michigan surveys usually ask if "there are any important differences in what the Republicans and Democrats stand for." There have been times when most Americans thought that there were, but by 1972, only 45 percent took this position; 46 percent disagreed, and 9 percent professed not to know. Pure Independents were found mostly in the "no" and "don't know" categories, as we would expect, and there was a clustering of Strong Republicans in the "yes" column. So far, so good. But nothing else is consistent with the proposition, as table 7.2 shows. People who thought there were important differences between the parties and people who thought not were distributed fairly evenly in the other five categories of party identifier. The results were similar for the years since 1972. By 1988, a healthy majority, 60 percent, thought that the parties differed meaningfully, and just 5 percent said they did not know.

The pattern of relationships, however, was pretty much the same as in 1972.

Perhaps we were casting our net too widely, including too many respondents who were wholly unconcerned about issues and opposing political philosophies. All Americans were not swept up in the tumult of the late 1960s. We might find something if we confined our analysis to respondents who cared enough about political ideas to acknowledge their own identity as liberals or conservatives. Because the United States has only two major parties, each inevitably is a broad coalition of interests and ideas. This may be particularly distasteful to people who favor principle over compromise. Such idealism is often thought to have reached a peak in the era we are examining, when all established institutions were questioned. We will examine the more general topic of alienation and dealignment in the next chapter. Here we focus on two possible specific manifestations: liberals' doubts that the Democratic party was liberal and a parallel refusal of conservatives to acknowledge that the Republican party shared their ideological proclivity.[17] The anguish of the liberals is a standard story about the period.

We begin with the standard NES question:

> We hear a lot of talk these days about liberals and conservatives. I'm going to show you a seven-point scale on which the political views that people might hold are arranged from extremely liberal to extremely conservative. Where would you place yourself on this scale, or haven't you thought much about this?

Twenty-eight percent of white respondents in 1972 said that they did not know where to place themselves or had not thought much about where they stood ideologically.[18] Another 27 percent put themselves at the "moderate, middle of the

17. There is no relation in the entire sample between strength of identification and responses to a question about whether one party is more conservative than the other.
18. The question about ideological self-identification was not asked until 1972.

road" midpoint of the scale. Pure Independents are most common in these two groups of nonideologues.

Although the remaining 45 percent of the respondents are interesting to us precisely for their ideological awareness, it is important to understand that people who call themselves conservatives may not take conservative positions on a particular issue, just as self-identified liberals may have views that cannot be called liberal. For example, 31 percent of those who called themselves liberals in 1972 preferred private to governmental solutions to the health-care problem, and 34 percent of self-identified conservatives favored federally funded health insurance plans. People who call themselves conservatives increasingly outnumber those who claim to be liberals, a trend that conflicts with stable or increasing liberal majorities on many specific policy questions.

The basic question about ideological self-identification was followed with requests that the respondent place various people and groups on the same seven-point scale. This series of items enables us to identify people who considered themselves liberals and then classify them according to their views of the Democratic party. In 1972, 34 percent of liberals did not consider the Democratic party liberal, compared to 31 percent in 1976 and 38 percent in 1988.

We can use these questions to test the proposition that liberals who deny the Democratic party's claim to liberalism will be more inclined to be Independents. Table 7.3 has the answers. It shows that in 1972, 26 percent of liberals who denied that the Democratic party shared their viewpoint were Independent Democrats, but so were 24 percent of the liberals who thought that the party passed muster ideologically. The comparison is almost identical for Weak Democrats. As the proposition predicts, Pure Independents were more common among liberals who rejected the party's credentials. The same pattern for Weak and Independent Democrats was found for 1976. The appeal of pure independence was even greater for liberals who rejected the Democratic party; 19 percent were

Table 7.3

Party Identification and Liberals' Views of the Democratic Party,
1972, 1976, and 1988

| | Is the Democratic Party Liberal?[a] | | | | | |
| | 1972 | | 1976 | | 1988 | |
	Yes	No	Yes	No	Yes	No
Strong Democrats	21%	16%	19%	8%	29%	25%
Weak Democrats	24	25	35	33	27	19
Indep. Democrats	24	26	22	21	20	28
Pure Independents	7	13	7	19	8	4
Indep. Republicans	9	11	7	11	6	5
Weak Republicans	10	7	8	6	7	16
Strong Republicans	5	3	3	3	4	4
	100%	101%	101%	101%	101%	101%
(N) =	(210)	(106)	(215)	(94)	(161)	(97)

[a]Description of the party's ideological position is by "placement" on the
seven-point scale used to measure the respondent's ideological self-
identification.

Pure Independents, compared to 7 percent of the liberals who
said the Democratic party was liberal.

In short, the data from the 1970s are discouraging with
respect to leaners but strongly support the proposition for
Pure Independents. The problem is that few liberals of any
sort are Pure Independents. As might be expected from what
we have seen about the political involvement of Pure Independents, they are less inclined than other varieties of identifier
to accept any sort of ideological label. In 1972, for example,
fully 63 percent of Pure Independents said that they had not
given much thought to their own ideological identity, or just
did not know how to respond to the question. Only 15 percent
of Pure Independents called themselves liberals. (We will discuss conservatives shortly.) The corresponding data for other

years are similar. What we have, then, is a promising clue about fewer than one-sixth of Pure Independents.

Table 7.3 also shows a trace of support for the basic proposition in 1988, half a generation after the tumult and disillusion that presumably bred the trend toward dealignment. In 1988 the proportion of liberals who questioned the Democratic party's liberalism was a bit higher, 38 percent, and the proportion of Democratic leaners in this group, 28 percent, was significantly higher than the 20 percent in the majority of liberals who granted that the Democratic party was liberal. On the other hand, now the distribution of Pure Independents becomes inconvenient. They were twice as common among liberals who accepted the Democratic party was liberal. Nevertheless, we have found another scrap of support for the proposition.

Conservatives usually have only bit parts in dramas about ideological conflict in the late 1960s when all the action was attributed to the left. Nevertheless, we thought it worthwhile to see if conservatives dissatisfied with the doctrinal adequacy of the Republican party might have contributed to dealignment. Table 7.4 shows the party identifications of conservatives, divided into those who did and those who did not consider the Republican party conservative. It shows absolutely no inclination toward being a Republican leaner among conservatives who doubted that the Republican party shared their ideological proclivity. In 1972 and 1988, these conservative doubters were more likely to be Pure Independents. As with the liberals, however, the significance of this relationship is limited by the modest number of conservatives of any sort who were Pure Independents: 22 percent in 1972 and 18 percent in 1988.

Table 7.4 also provides an interesting footnote: Conservatives who deny this label to the Republican party seem drawn to the Democratic party. This was true of 43 percent of the doubters in 1972, 46 percent in 1976, and just short of half in 1988. There was no such tendency among liberals.

Table 7.4
*Party Identification and Conservatives' Views of the Republican Party,
1972, 1976, and 1988*

| | Is the Republican Party Conservative?[a] | | | | | |
| | 1972 | | 1976 | | 1988 | |
	Yes	No	Yes	No	Yes	No
Strong Democrats	5%	7%	3%	13%	4%	15%
Weak Democrats	17	28	10	22	7	23
Indep. Democrats	6	8	5	11	4	11
Pure Independents	8	12	7	8	4	8
Indep. Republicans	17	15	20	16	20	17
Weak Republicans	25	15	25	19	23	13
Strong Republicans	22	15	31	12	39	13
	101%	100%	101%	101%	101%	100%
(N) =	(344)	(159)	(376)	(192)	(431)	(119)

[a]Description of the party's ideological position is by "placement" on the
seven-point scale used to measure the respondent's ideological self-
identification.

Evaluations of Political Groups

The political scene in the 1960s was enlivened by a variety of
new participants, from civil-rights workers to campus demon-
strators. Often these activists, rather than the causes they
advocated, were the main focus of public attention. We begin
by seeing how the seven types of party identifiers rated some
of these new groups on the feeling thermometer.

Six of the groups whose popularity was measured in the
Michigan surveys embodied aspects of the new politics: people who use marijuana, the women's liberation movement,
black militants, radical students, civil rights leaders, and people who riot in cities (the terms are those used in the question-

Table 7.5

Composite Feeling Thermometer Ratings of Six Liberal Reference Groups, by Age, 1972

| | Age | | | | All Respondents in Category |
	18–28	29–44	45–64	65+	
Strong Democrats	33	32	23	23	27
Weak Democrats	34	24	21	20	25
Indep. Democrats	43	29	28	25	35
Pure Independents	32	25	21	19	27
Indep. Republicans	31	25	19	23	26
Weak Republicans	32	25	20	17	23
Strong Republicans	25	22	17	16	19

Note: The six groups are marijuana users, women's liberationists, black militants, radical students, civil rights leaders, and urban rioters. Higher scores are more favorable.

naire). No one liked any of these people very much, but they were least unpopular among the Democratic leaners. Year after year, each of the groups got its warmest ratings from Independent Democrats, with outright Democratic partisans lagging behind. To be sure, young people were more sympathetic to these new forces, and Democratic leaners were disproportionately young. But differences among categories of identifiers generally remained when age was controlled. In other respects, however, these findings are disappointing. Neither Republican leaners nor Pure Independents looked more favorably on these groups than most other respondents. And even the younger Independent Democrats, although the least hostile, never approached neutrality, much less a kindly feeling. The ratings for 1972 are summarized in table 7.5. Scores for other years are similar.

Along with the debut of these new political actors came increased public attention to groups that had long been part of the political landscape and symbolized conservative values generally thought to be in conflict with the new politics. The

Table 7.6
Composite Feeling Thermometer Ratings of Three Conservative
Groups, by Age, 1972

	Age				All Respondents in Category
	18–28	*29–44*	*45–64*	*65+*	
Strong Democrats	59	63	71	73	68
Weak Democrats	60	66	70	73	67
Indep. Democrats	51	59	62	67	57
Pure Independents	59	68	70	64	65
Indep. Republicans	61	66	72	76	67
Weak Republicans	62	66	71	74	68
Strong Republicans	68	70	74	77	73

Note: The three groups are the police, the military, and big business. Higher scores are more favorable.

1972 ratings of three of these groups—the police, the military, and big business—are summarized in table 7.6. These groups were vastly more popular than the newer ones. Even the most liberal respondents, young Democratic leaners, felt more kindly toward these more conservative symbols than toward exemplars of the new politics. The conservative groups' ratings are almost a mirror image of what we saw in table 7.5. In 1972, Independent Democrats were somewhat cooler, Strong Republicans slightly warmer, and everyone else was in pretty much the same place. Pure Independents, rather than rejecting these old-fashioned groups, evaluated them much as the avowed partisans did. By 1988, feelings had cooled slightly almost across the board, the difference between Independent Democrats and others had narrowed, and only the Strong Republicans had views that diverged, however modestly, from the other six categories of partisanship.

Finally, we examined feelings about three groups that have traditionally been favored by liberals—labor unions, poor people, and people on welfare. These are symbols of bread-and-

Table 7.7

*Feeling Thermometer Ratings of Traditional Liberal
Symbols, 1976 and 1988*

	1976			1988		
	Labor unions	Poor people	People on welfare	Labor unions	Poor people	People on welfare
Strong Democrats	56	75	56	66	74	55
Weak Democrats	49	71	52	60	68	50
Indep. Democrats	47	70	51	57	68	49
Pure Independents	41	68	48	55	67	49
Indep. Republicans	42	68	46	48	65	46
Weak Republicans	43	69	47	48	65	46
Strong Republicans	37	69	47	44	67	44

Note: Higher scores are more favorable.

butter politics of the sort that was dismissed as obsolete by enthusiasts for the new issues of the 1960s. The results here alter the leaners' liberal image. As table 7.7 shows, Independent Democrats were cooler than Weak and Strong Democrats to unions, the poor, and welfare clients. On the Republican side, leaners had about the same views as outright partisans. Pure Independents were between Democrats and Republicans, closer to the latter. A secondary finding in table 7.7 is that opinion changed very little between 1976 and 1988 on the poor and people on welfare. Attitudes toward labor unions became generally more positive, especially for the three types of Democrats, Pure Independents, and Weak Republicans.

These findings sketch an emerging image of Independent Democrats: cooler toward traditional Democratic welfare constituencies and labor unions. Perhaps because of the decades that separate them from Depression-era worries, Democratic leaners, rather than being more liberal, are actually less favorably inclined toward these groups.

Attitudes on Public Policy

The Michigan researchers often measure opinions on issues by asking respondents to locate themselves on a seven-point scale extending between two extreme alternatives. This is an example of the format:

> Some people feel that the government in Washington should see to it that every person has a job and a good standard of living. Suppose that these people are at one end of this scale [card is shown to respondent]—at point number 1. Others think the government should just let each person get ahead on his own. Suppose that these people are at the other end—at point number 7. And, of course, some other people have opinions somewhere in between.
>
> Where would you place yourself on this scale, or haven't you thought much about this?

Table 7.8 displays the attitudes in 1972 of the seven types of identifier on a variety of life-style, civil-liberties, and racial issues. Several interesting generalizations are apparent. First, the range of opinion among Democrats, Independents, and Republicans is rather narrow, averaging just under one point on a seven-point scale. Second, although there is some tendency for Democrats to be to the left of the Republicans, there are many exceptions. Third, Democratic leaners are the most liberal on all but one issue. They are so much more liberal that on two issues—marijuana and protecting the rights of the accused—the gap between them and the next most liberal group is greater than the spread between the latter group and the rest of the sample. In view of the narrow range of variation generally, Independent Democrats are the only group who can be described as clearly and consistently different. To be sure, Strong Republicans always are at the most conservative position on any of the issues, but they are not the conspicuous outliers Independent Democrats are. Republican leaners, on the other hand, have a clearly different profile. On the first four issues in table 7.8, they are most liberal on regu-

Table 7.8

Attitudes on Life-style, Civil Liberties, and Racial Issues, 1972

	Regulate Industrial Pollution	Women's Equality	Legalize Marijuana	Protect Rights of Accused	Aid Minority Groups	Busing	Urban Unrest[a]
Strong Democrats	2.2	3.7	5.5	4.4	4.4	6.1	3.3
Weak Democrats	2.2	3.5	5.6	4.3	4.5	6.4	3.1
Indep. Democrats	2.0	3.0	4.3	3.4	3.9	6.1	2.7
Pure Independents	2.1	3.7	5.3	4.2	4.6	6.4	3.2
Indep. Republicans	1.7	3.3	5.2	4.2	4.5	6.5	3.3
Weak Republicans	2.3	3.6	5.4	4.5	4.5	6.5	3.3
Strong Republicans	2.6	3.7	5.8	4.8	4.8	6.7	3.6

Note: Based on responses to questions asking respondents to locate their position on a scale from 1 to 7, with 1 representing the most liberal position.

[a]The liberal option is "Correct the problems of poverty and unemployment that give rise to the disturbances." The other option is "Use all available force to maintain law and order."

Table 7.9

Attitudes on Traditional Social Welfare Issues, 1976

	Higher Taxes for the Rich	Government Guarantees Everyone a Job and a Good Standard of Living[a]	Federal Health Insurance
Strong Democrats	3.8	3.9	3.5
Weak Democrats	4.1	4.3	3.9
Indep. Democrats	4.1	4.4	3.4
Pure Independents	4.3	4.9	4.0
Indep. Republicans	4.4	4.9	4.5
Weak Republicans	4.5	4.9	4.6
Strong Republicans	4.7	5.4	5.1

Note: Lower scores are more liberal.
[a]Asked in the preelection interview.

lating pollution and in second place on the other three. On racial issues, however, they are on the more conservative side of the distribution. So many respondents are so opposed to busing that variations on this issue scarcely seem noteworthy. Our findings for other years are similar to those shown in table 7.8.

None of the preceding generalizations about attitudes on social questions holds for relationships between party identification and attitudes on economic issues. This proposition is conveniently illustrated by table 7.9, which displays relationships between party identification and preferences for higher taxes on the rich, government guarantees of well-being, and federal health insurance. Interparty differences are considerably greater and in no instance is any category of Democrat to the right of any kind of Republican. Moreover, Pure Independents always are in the middle. Finally, on two of these basic socioeconomic issues, there is an almost perfect monotonic relationship with party identification: as one moves from

Strong Democrat to Strong Republican, liberalism declines. On progressive taxation and guaranteed jobs the Strong Democrats are clearly the most liberal, followed by Weak Democrats, with Democratic leaners in third place. Much of the same is true on the Republican side. The coolness toward the New Deal tradition that was suggested by Democratic leaners' group ratings appears also in their middle-of-the-road preferences about economic issues, on which they are more conservative than their fellow partisans, with one exception, health insurance. This is also the only welfare-state issue we examined that is new, not a continuation of the New Deal agenda. The patterns displayed in table 7.9 occur in other years and on other economic issues.

Perceptions of Party Positions

These findings seem to tell a consistent story. Although not helpful about Pure Independents or Republican leaners, there are consistent hints about Democratic leaners: Being young and educated, neither memory, sentiment, nor self-interest made them receptive to the party-of-the-underdog image of the Democrats' New Deal–Fair Deal–Great Society tradition. They were interested in the problems of the late 1960s and early 1970s, not the 1930s. This might suggest that many call themselves Independents out of disappointment at the failure of either party's leaders to recognize their concerns and propose credible solutions.[19]

19. This picture of a sluggish Democratic leadership failing to respond to "new issues" hardly fits the situation in 1972 when George McGovern and the national convention delegates who nominated him were so preoccupied with new issues as to be out of touch with most Democrats. See Jeane Kirkpatrick, *The New Presidential Elite* (New York: Russell Sage Foundation and The Twentieth Century Fund, 1976), chap. 10. It is possible, of course, that the 1972-style incongruity contributed to the growth of a deviant breed of Democratic leaner who scorned radical chic and longed for the good old days of New Deal politics. The problem with this style of analysis is that one can always find examples of such incongruity, and thus *any* hypothesis about an unresponsive party would receive some support.

Many of the seven-point questions used by the NES to measure respondents' attitudes on issues also ask them to "place"
each of the parties on that issue. We can use these placements
to see to what extent respondents consider themselves in agreement with their party's position on most of the issues covered
in tables 7.8 and 7.9. That Independent Democrats are more
liberal than other Democrats on some issues and more conservative on others helps explain their avoidance of explicit identification with the party only if they think that the party is out of
step. If they see themselves in agreement with their party—or
no less so than outright partisans—it would not matter that
they are more liberal or conservative since these issues could
not be the cause of their independence.

Table 7.10 summarizes the gaps between our respondents'
positions on various issues and the position on each issue they
attribute to the Democratic party in 1972. Differences are
measured along the familiar seven-point scale. A positive
number indicates that the mean attitude of respondents in
that category is more liberal than their impressions of where
the Democratic party stands on the issue; that is, they see the
party to their right. A minus sign in table 7.10 indicates that
the position people in that category attribute to the Democratic party is to the left of their own position on that issue.

On the first three issues in table 7.10—regulating indus-
trial pollution, fighting inflation, and government health
insurance—Democratic leaners saw their party well to the
right of where they stood. On the first two of these issues,
however, the leaners' image of the party's position was the
same as that of Strong and Weak Democrats. They considered
the party slightly more conservative on women's equality and
urban unrest. But on the other issues, including those where
they were more liberal than other Democrats, Independent
Democrats either felt that their party was just about where
they were or that the party was *more* liberal than they. This is
true of life-style issues, as well as racial issues like busing and
unrest. These findings dampen the impulse to say that people
became Independent Democrats because they were too liberal

Table 7.10

Differences between Individuals' Positions on the Issues and the
Positions They Attribute to the Democratic Party, 1972

	Pollution	Inflation Policy[a]	Health Insurance	Women's Equality	Rights of Accused	Legalize Marijuana	Urban Unrest	Minority Aid	Busing
Strong Democrats	+0.7	+1.0	-0.3	-0.6	-0.7	-0.9	-0.3	-0.9	-1.7
Weak Democrats	+0.6	+0.8	-0.5	-0.4	-0.8	-1.1	+0.1	-1.1	-2.3
Indep. Democrats	+0.9	+0.9	+0.6	+0.3	+0.1	0.0	+0.3	-0.7	-1.9
Pure Independents	+0.4	+1.0	-0.9	-0.6	-0.7	-1.1	0.0	-1.3	-2.4
Indep. Republicans	+1.1	+1.2	-1.1	-0.3	-1.1	-1.4	-0.3	-1.7	-3.3
Weak Republicans	+0.4	+1.4	-1.8	-0.8	-1.3	-1.6	-0.2	-1.4	-3.0
Strong Republicans	+0.2	+1.5	-2.2	-0.8	-1.4	-1.9	-0.6	-1.8	-3.4

Note: Issue positions measured on a seven-point scale. A positive number indicates that respondents in that category have attributed a position to the Democratic party that is more conservative than their own position on the issue; a negative number shows that the Democratic party's position is thought to be further to the left.
[a]Asked in the preelection interview.

to fit in the Democratic party's mainstream; on most issues in 1972, Democratic leaners did not see themselves as more liberal than the party. In fact, in all years, they placed themselves closer to where they saw the party than did either Weak or Strong Democrats.[20]

The story is much the same for Independent Republicans. Perceptions in 1972 of the Republican party's positions on various issues are summarized in table 7.11. Only on pollution and inflation policy did Republican leaners consider themselves significantly more liberal than the Republican party and on the latter issue their image of the party was shared by outright Republican identifiers. On five other issues in table 7.11, Independent Republicans were closer to where they saw their party than were other Republicans.[21]

Neither table 7.10 nor table 7.11 sheds much light on Pure Independents, whose impressions of the parties' stands on the issues were generally midway between those of the partisans.

We have narrowed our search for the causes of dealignment to those issues where there are substantial gaps between leaners' beliefs and those they attribute to the parties. Could these issues—pollution and health insurance—be the focus of leaners' dissatisfaction with the two parties? Have we found the causes of the parties' decline? Can we conclude that those issues on which leaners consider themselves at odds with their party are partly responsible for dealignment?

People whose party identification is affected by their beliefs about an issue should consider that issue important. At this point, the line of analysis we have been pursuing peters out: People who are particularly interested in any of the areas where leaners are at odds with their party have no distinctive

20. In 1988 the differences were not very great between Independent Democrats and other Democrats in the extent to which they saw themselves as more liberal or more conservative than the Democratic party. The differences were largest on the issues of cooperation with the Soviet Union and women's rights.

21. In 1988 Independent Republicans and Weak Republicans were strikingly similar in their positioning of themselves and their party, usually within one point on the seven-point scale.

Table 7.11

Differences between Individuals' Positions on the Issues and the
Positions They Attribute to the Republican Party, 1972

	Pollution	Inflation Policy[a]	Health Insurance	Women's Equality	Rights of Accused	Legalize Marijuana	Urban Unrest	Minority Aid	Busing
Strong Democrats	+0.9	+1.7	+1.3	−0.1	0.0	−0.5	+1.0	−0.2	−1.5
Weak Democrats	+0.9	+1.2	+0.6	0.0	−0.2	−0.3	+0.8	−0.2	−0.3
Indep. Democrats	+1.8	+1.5	+1.9	+1.0	+0.8	+1.0	+1.5	+0.4	−1.4
Pure Independents	+0.5	+1.1	+0.6	−0.3	−0.4	0.0	+0.5	−0.6	−1.6
Indep. Republicans	+1.1	+0.6	+0.1	−0.1	−0.3	−0.1	+0.3	−0.5	−1.3
Weak Republicans	−0.4	+0.7	−0.2	−0.4	−0.3	−0.3	+0.3	−0.5	−1.4
Strong Republicans	0.0	+0.4	−0.2	−0.5	−0.6	−0.3	−0.1	−0.8	−1.4

Note: Issue positions measured on a seven-point scale. A positive number indicates that respondents in that category have attributed a position to the Republican party that is more conservative than their own position on the issue; a negative number shows that the Republican party's position is thought to be further to the left.
[a]Asked in the preelection interview.

preference for any level of partisanship. Indeed, we can be more categorical: Analysis of respondents' ideas about "the most important problem the country faces" reveals no tendency for people most concerned with any category of problem to be leaners, avowed partisans, or Pure Independents.

A second finding deals another blow to the issue-disparity argument. Tables 7.10 and 7.11 show that very often it was strong or weak partisans who were most out of step with their party. They, not leaners, often had more reason to be upset. On many issues, leaners were closer than outright partisans to where they saw their party standing.

We saw earlier that self-identified liberals' and conservatives' views of the ideological place of the two parties provided only very limited help in explaining dealignment. When we examine the ideological images of the two parties held by all respondents, we find, as was the case with issues, that leaners are at least as likely as outright partisans to see their party in step with them ideologically.

A Constituency for a Third Party?

In the view of some scholars and other observers, one clear implication of the growth of Independents was that as "the largest group in the society," they formed "a large pool of nonimmunized citizens . . . available for mobilization to new partisan commitments."[22] George Gallup considered the possibilities this way:

> With independents moving toward a dominant role in American politics, candidates of both major parties will by vying for their votes as the 1976 presidential race begins to take shape. . . . independents could provide a base for a third-party effort in the coming months. . . . independents could form the basis of a "centrist" party

22. Nie, Verba, and Petrocik, *The Changing American Voter*, 346, 94.

much like parties in other nations, taking a position midway between the right and left.[23]

Six years later, the *New York Times* drew on Gallup Poll data about the number of Independents to speculate along similar lines:

> There is talk about an independent movement, a Center Party, a Third Force, made up of people unsatisfied with both sides of a Carter-Reagan race.... There is a rational base for such a grouping. In recent years, analysts have identified a large and growing corps of voters located between the major parties.[24]

Walter Dean Burnham, on the other hand, thought that survey data suggested a very different possibility, a constituency for a left-wing party:

> The exceptionally rapid erosion of the behavioral hold of the old major parties on the American electorate which is now going on may be part of a prealignment process during which masses of voters become available for mobilization along other than traditional lines.[25]

Such speculations assume that there is only one type of Independent, not three. If all three kinds of Independents are combined, then they seem to be a middle-of-the-road constituency because Republican and Democratic leaners offset each other and in the aggregate resemble the genuinely neutral Pure Independents. But as tables 7.8 and 7.9 show, the range of opinion among the three kinds of Independents is fully as broad as in the whole population. There is no policy issue on

23. George Gallup, "The Nation's Independents—Now a Possible Base for a New Party," The Gallup Poll release, November 17, 1974, 1. Ten years later, Everett Carll Ladd, Jr., characterized Independents' attitudes this way: "No Distinctive Ideological Outlook on Issues." See his "Declarations of Independents," *Public Opinion*, April–May 1984, 24.
24. *The New York Times*, March 20, 1980, A26.
25. Walter Dean Burnham, *Critical Elections and the Mainsprings of American Politics* (New York: W. W. Norton, 1970), 92.

which they are any more united than the entire American white population. This should put to rest the fanciful notion that Independents are a constituency for a third party that will appeal to people who consider the Democratic party too liberal and the Republican party too conservative.

Since Independents are so diverse, it is difficult to imagine them rallying behind a major third party offering any alternative set of policies. The followers of the two established parties do not display much consensus on the issues either. But affiliation with Democrats or Republicans is rooted in a rich history, full of meaningful associations and symbols. These histories are products of critical change, when one or the other party took a distinctive approach to a consuming problem. So far, no such issue has provided a focus for Independents; not economic policy, new moral conceptions, ecological concerns, nor race relations. If such an issue does arise, it is likely to affect the American political consciousness in a way completely different from that suggested by present conceptions.

Party identification is an important concept to the extent that it explains behavior—vote choice, attitudes, whatever— that is worthy of explanation. In the language of social science, it is valued as an independent variable. This is not to say, however, that it cannot be explained, that is, be treated as a dependent variable. Since the beginning of chapter 6 we have done this in searching for understanding of the undeniable increase in Independents that began in the late 1960s. The major theme of this book is that this increase generally has been misinterpreted because of a widespread failure to differentiate leaners from Pure Independents.

We have not been very successful in tying the increase in any variety of Independent to the great issues of the late 1960s and early 1970s. With one exception, we have failed to make a case for attributing dealignment to a belief that the parties do not offer meaningful alternatives. By the same token, we have found that ideologues dissatisfied with the doctrinal vagueness of the two parties were not responsible for dealignment.

The exception just alluded to concerns the concentration of

Pure Independents in the ranks of citizens who questioned that the major parties really differ from each other. In chapter 5, when we were describing Independents instead of trying to explain them, we found that Pure Independents were likelier to think that the parties did not differ in their ability to perform satisfactorily on the most important problem. Are some Americans Pure Independents because they take the European view that Republicans and Democrats are like two peas in a pod? Or should we expect that people who persevere in denying any affinity for either party will see the world that way, even when the parties are led by men as different as Richard Nixon and George McGovern or Ronald Reagan and Walter Mondale?

At some stage in the search for independent variables that differentiate Independents from outright partisans, common sense will intervene to suggest that irrespective of some observed relationship, it is not plausible to attribute dealignment to it. For example, if we found that feeling thermometer ratings of "people who live in suburbs" or "ministers who lead protest marches" neatly sorted out Independent Democrats from Weak and Strong Democrats, we would not believe that we had discovered the elusive key to dealignment. The point of these last three paragraphs is to announce that we have arrived at that stage. We acknowledge our failure to locate the issues that led to the growth of Independents.

8

Alienation and Independence

We saw in the last chapter that the new issues of the late 1960s and early 1970s were not responsible for the growth of Independents. Here we examine the possibility that it was not specific issues but the widely remarked loss of faith in politicians and the political system itself that led to dealignment. Many writers noted the concurrent increases in alienation and independence, and attributed the latter to the former. Frustration at so many problems, coupled with a belief that the government did not or could not find solutions, presumably led millions of people to reject affiliation with a party, just as they rejected other elements of the American creed.[1] Most of the scholars who made the connection between alienation and dealignment did not differentiate the three varieties of Independents. Because this grouping was so large—and presumably so devoid of partisan anchors—its disaffection was considered a potential threat to the continued stability of the political system.

The era was neither calm nor happy. One political scientist

1. Blacks exceeded whites in the extent and durability of their increased political discontent but did not share in the parallel trend toward weakened partisanship, as we saw in chapter 2.

began a 1969 article on "The End of American Party Politics" with the observation that "American politics has clearly been falling apart in the past decade."[2] Another scholar found that "a situation of widespread, basic discontent and political alienation exists in the U.S. today."[3] The study of political discontent became a growth industry, soon producing a substantial body of largely inconclusive research.[4] Various measures of discontent all rose during the period and remained near peak levels long after demonstrations and political violence had subsided. For example, the proportion of Americans scoring "high" or "medium" on the Michigan political-trust index (see Appendix) fell from 72 percent in 1964 to 64 percent in 1968, and 50 percent in 1972, and then to about a third for the rest of the decade.[5]

One consequence of this trend was thought to be the increase in Independents.

> The new issues that arose in the 1960s . . . caused substantial discontent. They led the public to turn against the political parties and the political process more generally. . . . The result of the new issues is weakened

2. Walter Dean Burnham, "The End of American Party Politics," *Transaction* 7 (December 1969): 12.

3. Arthur H. Miller, "Political Issues and Trust in Government," *American Political Science Review* 68 (September 1974): 951.

4. For a useful summary of the literature in the heyday of this specialty, see Edward N. Muller and Thomas O. Jukam, "On the Meaning of Political Support," *American Political Science Review* 71 (December 1977): 1561–95.

5. Paul R. Abramson and Ada W. Finifter, "On the Meaning of Political Trust: New Evidence from Items Introduced in 1978," *American Journal of Political Science* 25 (May 1981): 297. Confidence in government rebounded in Reagan's first term, although not back to the levels characteristic of pre-Vietnam days. See especially Jack Citrin and Donald Philip Green, "Presidential Leadership and the Resurgence of Trust in Government," *British Journal of Political Science* 16 (October 1986): 431–53. Political trust declined again after 1984, however. See Arthur H. Miller and Stephen A. Borrelli, "Confidence in Government during the 1980s," *American Politics Quarterly* 19 (April 1991): 147–72.

commitment to parties and politics, not reconstituted commitments.[6]

It seems that the significant decrease in party identification, coupled with the decrease in voting and the use of less conventional avenues of political expression and protest, indicate a sense of political disquiet that is both deep and widespread.[7]

Disenchanted with government and politics, many identified as independents as a way of registering their disapproval.[8]

Increasing alienation and more Independents characterized the era of the late 1960s and early 1970s. Scholars who linked these developments seem to have succumbed to the appeal of the parallel trend: If two changes occur more or less simultaneously, one must cause the other. It must have seemed perfectly logical to conclude that distrust of institutions would lead to less affiliation with such prominent institutions as the two major parties. The plausibility of this link evidently was such that few who wrote like the ones quoted presented data on this putative relationship. We will consider exceptions to this generalization after a closer look at various kinds of distrust.

Dimensions of Alienation

The study of alienation bridges two centuries and several academic disciplines. Considerable effort has been expended on defining alienation, explicating various aspects, and searching for their causes and consequences. Empirically oriented political scientists discern at least three distinct varieties of

6. Norman H. Nie, Sidney Verba, and John R. Petrocik, *The Changing American Voter*, enlarged ed. (Cambridge: Harvard University Press, 1979), 350.
7. Richard E. Dawson, *Public Opinion and Contemporary Disarray* (New York: Harper and Row, 1973), 5.
8. Abraham Holtzman, *American Government*, 2d ed. (Englewood Cliffs, N.J.: Prentice-Hall, 1984), 139.

alienation: powerlessness, distrust, and doubt about governmental responsiveness.[9]

Powerlessness is measured by some or all of the four agree-disagree items in the NES political efficacy scale. A sample efficacy item: "Voting is the only way that people like me can have any say about how the government runs things."[10] Distrust is measured by five questions, exemplified by this one: "Would you say the government is pretty much run by a few big interests looking out for themselves or that it is run for the benefit of all the people?" Doubts that political institutions are responsive to ordinary voters are measured by questions like this one: "How much do you feel that political parties help to make the government pay attention to what the people think: a good deal, some, or not much?" The National Election Studies items that tap these three dimensions are in the Appendix.

Study of political support has been dogged by the difficulty of differentiating approval of the political system and of the incumbent administration. The self-evident theoretical importance of this distinction has been elaborated by theorists,[11] but empirical researchers have not seemed altogether successful in making the point to respondents, who persist in viewing the American political order through a partisan screen. When a Democrat was president, Strong Republicans were the most

9. This typology is from Robert Gilmour and Robert Lamb, *Political Alienation in Contemporary America* (New York: St. Martin's Press, 1975).

10. This item and the one about politics seeming too complicated for "a person like me" to understand have come to be called the *internal efficacy* index because they appear to tap the individual's sense of his own capacity. The other two items in the index in the Appendix are thought to measure *external efficacy,* belief in the effect of ordinary citizens' wishes on what the government does. This distinction is not crucial for our analysis.

11. The most widely cited example is David Easton, *A Systems Analysis of Political Life* (New York: John Wiley and Sons, 1965). Easton found it useful to introduce *specific* and *diffuse* as synonyms for *incumbent* and *system.*

cynical and Strong Democrats the most trusting; with a Republican in the White House, these relationships were reversed.[12] Try as they might to devise questions that would measure "feelings about the legitimacy of the system of political authority as a whole" as opposed merely to approval of the administration's performance, researchers reported that "separate indicators of these analytical constructs generally are found to be highly correlated."[13] The authors of a determined effort to resolve this dilemma concluded that "trust in government is . . . more sensitive to incumbent than to system affect and should be classified in the same category as such variables as evaluation of public policy outputs and general approval-disapproval of the performance of an incumbent administration."[14]

Because answers to questions about the political system reflect in substantial degree the respondent's partisan inclinations, use of the inclusive measure of independence raises the problem of aggregation we have discussed throughout this book. Any attempt to relate alienation to the growing number of Independents requires separating leaners from Pure Independents and subdividing them into Democrats and Republicans. Otherwise, disparate responses by the three varieties of Independents may aggregate into a misleadingly neutral pattern. This is sufficient to explain an early finding that Independents did not differ significantly from partisans with respect to political efficacy or "their assessments of how attentive the

12. An early and detailed demonstration of this relationship is in Jack Citrin, "Comment: Political Issues and Trust in Government," *American Political Science Review* 68 (September 1974): 976–78. For a summary of later research making the same point, see William Schneider, "Antipartisanship in America," in *Parties and Democracy in Britain and America*, ed. Vernon Bogdanor (New York: Praeger, 1984), 108–10. Citrin and Green's analysis shows that the most important independent variable of political trust is not party identification but approval of the president's performance in office. See their "Presidential Leadership."

13. Muller and Jukam, "Meaning of Political Support," 1562, 1563.

14. Ibid., 1589.

government is to public opinion . . . or the attentiveness of the members of Congress."[15]

On the other hand, another study that also combined all types of Independents came to the opposite conclusion:

> It should come as no surprise that the alienated Americans are independent in their politics; they're not likely to claim membership in either of the two major political parties. The national election surveys . . . consistently report that increasing numbers of disillusioned and politically estranged voters declined to state a party preference.[16]

Try as we might, we were unable to replicate these findings.

A third relevant study did differentiate leaners and Pure Independents. No relationship was found between cynicism and "strength of partisanship," but the party identification choices of more- and less-alienated respondents were not reported.[17]

Our findings can be briefly told: Relationships between party identification and various measures of alienation are unimpressive at best. In 1970, 16 percent of the least trusting and 9 percent of the most trusting (each group was about a fifth of all white respondents) were Pure Independents. On the other hand, there were no differences in 1972, 1974, and 1976. Our findings for efficacy are similar: differences in the predicted direction in some years, none at all in others. In 1976, for example, 9 percent of those at the top of the efficacy scale

15. Dennis S. Ippolito and Thomas Walker, *Political Parties, Interest Groups, and Public Policy* (Englewood Cliffs, N.J.: Prentice-Hall, 1980), 125, 128.

16. Gilmour and Lamb, *Political Alienation*, 122.

17. Martin P. Wattenberg, "The Decline of Political Partisanship in the United States: Negativity or Neutrality?" *American Political Science Review* 75 (December 1981): 943–44. Wattenberg found a similar absence of a relation between changes in political trust and strength of party identification in panels of young and middle-aged respondents interviewed in 1965 and 1973. See his *The Decline of American Political Parties, 1952–1984* (Cambridge: Harvard University Press, 1986), 55–57.

Table 8.1

Party Identification of People with Most and Least Trust in Government, 1972

	SD	WD	ID	I	IR	WR	SR	% of Sample
Least trusting	16	24	15	17	8	12	9	21
Most trusting	14	19	13	15	11	19	10	21

(12 percent of whites) and 18 percent of the least efficacious were Pure Independents. The same was true in 1970, while in 1974 there was no difference. The third component of alienation, a belief in the government's responsiveness, performs in the same way. In 1974 nearly a third of the highly alienated on this dimension were Pure Independents, compared to 10 percent of the most satisfied. In 1972 the corresponding figures were 20 and 13 percent, and in 1970, no pattern was found.

Because dealignment was most common among the young, we analyzed the effect of alienation separately for the four age groups examined in chapter 6. Briefly stated, we found that in 1968 and 1972 the relationships to partisan neutrality of mistrust and disbelief in governmental responsiveness were a bit stronger for respondents under 29 than for the entire sample. The strongest relationship of mistrust to pure independence, however, was in the oldest age group, those 65 and older.

Table 8.1 displays the party identification of the most and least trusting people in 1972. It shows no tendency for the mistrustful to eschew partisanship. There is a modest difference in table 8.2, which charts party identification and belief in the responsiveness of political institutions; here the gap between most and least alienated is seven percentage points in the predicted direction.

In short, sometimes there is a tendency for respondents who are most disenchanted with the political system (or with those who are currently running it) to be Pure Independents.

Table 8.2
*Party Identification of People with Most and Least Belief in
Government Responsiveness, 1972*

	SD	WD	ID	I	IR	WR	SR	% of Sample
Government is responsive	13	18	10	13	13	18	16	22
Government is unresponsive	14	27	13	20	10	11	6	24

But there is no such relationship for leaners. The most and least alienated are equally likely to be leaners, on either the Democratic or Republican side and on both components of alienation. The same was found in other years. Simply put, there is no relationship at all between any measure of political alienation and partisan independence.

Beyond Alienation

In addition to the widely discussed indexes on trust, efficacy, and belief in responsiveness, the NES has also asked questions intended to measure a more thoroughgoing dissatisfaction with the basic political system. Relatively little attention has been paid to these items, perhaps because the number who reject the system is so small that few cases are available for analysis. One question asks whether "a change in our whole form of government is needed to solve the problems facing our country." A second inquires whether the respondent can find much in "our form of government to be proud of." A third asks whether the country is "in good shape" or "something is very wrong." The last of these items was asked only in 1972. As expected, people who took a dim view of the country's condition were more likely to be Democrats, but there was no other discernible relationship with any category of party identification.

Answers to the question about whether one could be proud

of "our form of government" were related to partisanship—with Ford or Nixon in the White House, pride and Republicanism went together—but also to political context; 17 percent acknowledged lack of pride in 1976, compared to 12 percent before Watergate. In either year, the proud majority was a bit less likely to be Pure Independent than the unproud minority: 13 compared to 20 percent in 1972, 14 and 21 percent in 1976. As usual, there was no relationship for leaners.

The question about "a big change . . . in our form of government" yielded an almost identical pattern of responses. Nineteen percent favored a big change in 1972 and 24 percent in 1976. The advocates of change were mostly Democrats; there was no relationship with leaners; and Pure Independents were half again as common among the big-change group as in those who wanted to stand pat or only "some change."

Having said this much, we think it important to note that none of these findings is much help in explaining dealignment. At most, one-fifth of the most fundamentally disaffected were Independents without any inclination toward a party. If thoroughgoing rejection of our political system were the cause of independence, we would expect far higher proportions of the disenchanted to be Pure Independents.

Summary

In chapter 7 we investigated the impact of some specific issues of the 1960s and 1970s on the likelihood that a person would be an Independent. Contrary to the speculations of many, none of the most salient issues of the period seems to have stimulated dealignment. In this chapter we have examined the possibility that alienation from the political process, or at least from those in power, led to the rise of Independents in the period.

We have uncovered little evidence in support of the notion that a fundamental rejection of the political system led to the increase. Not only were most people basically supportive of the government and the political process during the entire period studied, but those most alienated from the system accounted for only a small portion of the increase in Pure Independents. Our finding that political alienation is modestly related to independence refers only to Pure Independents. We could find no evidence that alienation or frustration with politics led to partisan independence.

9

Alternatives

Our search for the sources of the increase in Independents has been largely fruitless. We have seen that general political discontent was not very helpful in explaining the trend, except in a limited way for Pure Independents. The same is true for beliefs about the lack of meaningful differences between the parties. In the latter case, of course, there is no way to be sure which way the causation runs. People who decline two invitations to align themselves with either party might be expected to say that those parties do not offer consequential alternatives.

We have also seen that leaners' choices of candidates and their attitudes toward the parties justify our label for them—closet partisans. But despite their affinity for one party, leaners like to think of themselves as something other than partisans. It is not just that they call themselves Independents; they prize that identity sufficiently to suffer patterned failures of memory when reporting their past behavior. Explanations of this phenomenon are not evident. As Jack Dennis observed, the accumulated wisdom of political science "still does not answer the question of why closet partisans find it convenient or compelling to call themselves Independents."[1]

1. Jack Dennis, "Political Independence in America, Part II: Towards a Theory," *British Journal of Political Science* 18 (April 1988): 202.

Growing doubts about the measurement of party identification put this topic high on the agenda when assured financial support enabled the National Election Studies to give sustained attention to measurement problems in the late 1970s. A conference on party identification in early 1978 initiated a process of discussion and innovation that included a 1979 pilot study and culminated in batteries of new items on parties in the 1980 NES questionnaire. These achievements reflected two ideas that we will explore here: (1) attitudes toward parties as such may explain the proliferation of Independents; (2) the familiar Michigan questions about party identification tapped opinions about independence as well as the Democratic and Republican parties and thus were measuring two distinct phenomena in a one-dimensional index.

Attitudes toward Parties

We noted in chapter 1 that political parties are not very popular with most Americans. Nothing we say here contradicts this general impression, although we will see that there are limits to public willingness to express hostility to the parties. This was apparent in responses to the only question the NES asked in 1968 about political parties: "How much do you feel that political parties help to make the government pay attention to what the people think?" Thirty-nine percent of whites replied "a good deal," 43 percent said "some," and just 18 percent answered "not much." More important for our current concern is the finding that there were no differences in the distribution of party identifiers among these three attitudes. In 1970, on the other hand, Pure Independents were twice as common among the skeptics (who now accounted for an even fifth of whites), and Democratic leaners were somewhat scarcer in the affirmative group.

The 1972 questionnaire included this question:

Which of the parts of the government on this list [the respondent is handed a card with "Congress," "the Supreme Court," "the President," and "the political parties"] do you think has done the best job in the past couple of years?

Eventually the respondent discloses his or her candidate for the worst job. This sequence was followed by an inquiry leading up to a question about which of the four was "least powerful," and then by a third series eventuating in a question asking which "you least often trust to do what's right?" Fifty-two percent named the parties for "worst job," 73 percent for "least powerful," and 69 percent considered them least trusted "to do what's right." These findings are consistent with expectations about the parties' low place in public esteem, even when compared to such frequently derided institutions as Congress and the Supreme Court. More surprising, perhaps, is the absence of any tendency for strong partisans to be notably scarce, or Independents more numerous, in the ranks of those with negative views of the parties. Controlling for age did not alter this result.

In addition to the carefully planned new questions on attitudes toward the parties, which we will examine shortly, the 1980 questionnaire included a battery of questions about "how good a job you feel some of the parts of our government are doing." Perhaps because this series asked for an evaluation of each part separately rather than in comparison with all the others, the parties came off somewhat better than in 1972. A third felt that the parties were doing a poor job; another third put them at the middle of the nine-point rating scale, "fair job;" 18 percent were on the favorable side of this midpoint; and the rest said they did not know. As in 1972, however, this question did not at all differentiate partisans and Independents, except that a greater proportion of Pure Independents were in the "don't know" category.

"Political parties, in general" was an item on the feeling thermometer in 1980. Nine percent said they could not make a judgment. Of those who did, 20 percent rated parties unfavorably, another 30 percent put them at the neutral 50-degree mark, and the remainder were on the favorable side.[2] Those who rated parties favorably were somewhat more likely to be outright partisans, but the relationships were neither consistent nor robust. The same was true in 1984.

One of the major innovations in 1980 was a set of questions designed to measure attitudes toward political parties as institutions, without regard to a particular party. The items were in the form of statements with which respondents were asked to express their agreement or disagreement on a seven-point scale. The questions are in table 9.1, which also classifies responses to each statement as pro-party, balanced (the midpoint on the seven-point scale), and anti-party. Omitted are "don't know" responses, which ranged from 2 to 7 percent of white respondents.

Several scholars have used these questions as dependent variables, presenting the scores on each question, or on an index of all of them, of strong partisans, weak partisans, and Independents, either combined or separately for leaners.[3] Our approach is different. For one thing, if different appraisals of parties explain why some people choose to be leaners rather than weak partisans, then party identification, not party support, is the dependent variable. Second, at any given level of strength, Republicans and Democrats differ in their attitudes toward parties; hence, combining them conceals a finding that should be displayed. Third, we cannot take the second item in table 9.1 seriously. How could understanding the appeal of calling oneself an Independent be enhanced by learn-

2. The midpoints in these two scales were presented somewhat differently to respondents. On the feeling thermometer, a 50-degree reading represents neutrality; on the job-rating scale, the midpoint designates a judgment: the parties are doing a "fair job."

3. Stephen C. Craig, "Partisanship, Independence, and No Preference: Another Look at the Measurement of Party Identification," *American Journal of Political Science* 29 (May 1985): 278; William Schneider, "Antipartisanship in America," in *Parties and Democracy in Britain and America,* ed. Vernon Bogdanor (New York: Praeger, 1984), 104–5; Martin P. Wattenberg, *The Decline of American Political Parties 1952–1984* (Cambridge: Harvard University Press, 1986), 15–17.

Table 9.1

Party Support Questions, 1980

	Pro-party (%)	Balanced (%)	Anti-party (%)
The best rule in voting is to pick a candidate regardless of party label.	17	8	75
It is better to be a firm party supporter than to be a political independent.	29	13	58
The parties do more to confuse the issues than to provide a clear choice on issues.	23	21	57
It would be better if, in all elections, we put no party labels on the ballot.	38	12	50
The truth is we probably don't need political parties in America anymore.	57	11	32

ing that very few Independents of any variety agree that it is better not to be an Independent?[4] Fourth, we accepted the textbook injunction that it is preferable to measure a variable with several items rather than a single question and therefore analyzed responses to the questions in table 9.1 in order to build a satisfactory scale.

Cronbach's alpha coefficient of reliability is higher for the last three items in table 9.1 than for all five items or for all but the second item: .72 for the last three, .68 for all five, and .67 for all but the second.[5] We created a simple additive anti-

4. For the record, we report that 13 Independent Democrats, 19 Pure Independents, and 16 Independent Republicans agreed that it is better not to be a political independent.

5. Lee J. Cronbach, "Coefficient Alpha and the Internal Structure of Tests," *Psychometrika* 16 (1951): 297–334. These three items, together with the feeling thermometer measure of "political parties, in general," formed Dennis's "antipartisanship" dimension identified

party scale by summing each respondent's score on each of the last three questions. The low point on the scale is three, indicating a respondent who chose to "disagree very strongly" with each of the three statements. The top score of 21 goes to anyone who expressed maximum agreement with each of the three anti-party statements.

The variation among the seven types of party identifier was predictable but surprisingly narrow, as table 9.2 shows. Strong Republicans and Democrats were least hostile to the parties, at 10.1 and 10.2, respectively. On the Democratic side, the gap between strong and weak partisans, 2.2 points, is slightly greater than the difference between Weak Democrats and Independent Democrats, 1.8 points. Pure Independents were almost identical to Democratic leaners, but the gap between Pure Independents and Republican leaners, 1.3 points, is almost as great as the difference between the latter group and Weak Republicans, who in turn were 1.5 points higher on antipartisanship than Strong Republicans. In short, although our measure of antipartisanship differentiated all three kinds of Independents from outright partisans, it did at least as good a job distinguishing between strong and weak partisans.

Dennis's analysis produced an even more emphatic version of the same pattern. His "anti-partyism" index included our three items plus reversed feeling thermometer scores for political parties. The percentage of each category of party identifier who scored high on his index is also displayed in table 9.2. Dennis's and our findings lead us to question both Schneider's conclusion that "Calling oneself an Independent is, in short, an expression of antipartisanship," and Wattenberg's report (based on combining Democrats and Republicans) that there are "no significant differences" between leaners and Pure Independents.[6]

---

by principal-component analysis of a total of fifteen relevant items in the 1980 NES questionnaire. See Dennis, "Political Independence, Part II," 206–7.

6. Schneider, "Antipartisanship in America," 105; Wattenberg, *The Decline of American Political Parties*, 16.

Table 9.2
Party Identification and Anti-party Attitudes, 1980

	Mean Score on Our Anti-party Scale[a]	Percent High on Dennis Anti-partyism Index[b]
Strong Democrats	10.2	15
Weak Democrats	12.4	34
Indep. Democrats	14.2	47
Pure Independents	14.3	49
Indep. Republicans	13.0	40
Weak Republicans	11.6	27
Strong Republicans	10.1	16

[a]The anti-party scale is based on agreement with the last three items in table 9.1 and ranges from 3 to 21.
[b]From Dennis, "Political Independence in America, Part II," 211.

These observations are preliminaries to the main event, our attempt to see if hostility to political parties helps explain leaners' aversion to accepting a partisan identity. We started with a 19 × 7 matrix, plotting the distribution of party identification among respondents with each possible score on our anti-party scale from 3 to 21. A general pattern was evident, but there were so many anomalous cells that we settled for a tripartite division, based on inspection of the matrix, that seemed to yield the greatest differentiation of the seven types of identifier. The high-support group, amounting to about a quarter of the sample, included those scoring from 3 to 8 on the scale. The low-support group, of about equal size, was those who had scores from 16 to 21. The rest, nearly half the respondents, are the modest-support group. The complete cross-tabulation is in table 9.3.

Some of the relations in table 9.3 are strongly in the predicted direction. Over three-quarters of those in the high-support group are outright partisans, as are 62 percent of those in the middle and just under half of the low supporters.

Table 9.3

Support for Parties and Party Identification, 1980

	High Support[a]	Modest Support[b]	Low Support[c]
Strong Democrats	22%	13%	7%
Weak Democrats	22	22	24
Indep. Democrats	7	11	19
Pure Independents	7	13	20
Indep. Republicans	8	13	13
Weak Republicans	18	17	13
Strong Republicans	15	10	5
	99%	99%	101%
(N) =	(309)	(569)	(331)

[a]Respondents who scored from 3 to 8 on a scale of the last three questions in table 9.1.
[b]Respondents with scores from 9 to 15 on the anti-party scale.
[c]Respondents with scores from 16 to 21 on the anti-party scale.

By the same token, there is no difference between Pure Independents and leaners except for the low-support column, in which Republican leaners are a bit underrepresented. That's the good news. Closer inspection reveals that most of the relationship between support for the parties and outright partisanship reflects strong identifiers. On both the Republican and the Democratic sides, the proportion of strong partisans in the high-support column is at least three times as great as among low supporters. On the other hand, about equal proportions of Weak Democrats appear in all three groups, and differences among Weak Republicans amount to just five percentage points.

We conclude that doubts about the parties as institutions have something to do with dealignment. We would be more confident about saying this if similar data on support for parties were available for other years and if the more sketchy data from earlier years had yielded findings that were consistent with the proposition.

The Dimensionality of Party Identification

Does calling oneself an Independent necessarily exclude identifying as a Democrat or Republican?

> A basic concern here is whether a person can identify with more than one group. Multiple identifications certainly exist, as when people consider themselves both Americans and Catholics. Yet, identification with one group generally seems to preclude identification with opposite groups.[7]

The question, then, is whether "political independence is just the opposite of partisanship."[8] The NES party identification question assumed that it was—that independence was simply the null or balance point of a single continuum extending from Democratic to Republican identification. Partisanship and independence may not be mutually exclusive, however. It is possible that they coexist in the same individual because instead of being merely the absence of partisanship, independence has a separate, positive character.

David Valentine and John Van Wingen applied this idea to identify those areas of belief and behavior in which they thought leaners should be more partisan than weak identifiers, equally partisan, or less partisan. Where overt partisan affect was involved, in evaluations of the parties and reported consistency of voting for one party's candidates, leaners' independence should cause them to be less partisan than weak identifiers. With less overtly partisan perspectives and behavior, such as feelings of political efficacy, interest in politics or the current campaign, or media usage, the leaners' independence should cause them to be more active and therefore "more partisan than the weak partisans."[9] Finally, on "orienta-

7. Herbert F. Weisberg, "A Multidimensional Conceptualization of Party Identification," *Political Behavior* 2 (1980): 34.
8. Ibid., 34.
9. David C. Valentine and John R. Van Wingen, "Partisanship, Independence, and the Partisan Identification Question," *American Politics Quarterly* 8 (April 1980): 170.

tions toward specific elections," monotonicity should not be expected. Therefore leaners and weak identifiers should be equally partisan in their preference for one or the other presidential candidate and their concern about the outcome. Finding confirmation for all three propositions, Valentine and Van Wingen concluded that a two-dimensional conceptualization of party identification, taking into account the separate effect of independence, explained the "seemingly peculiar behavior of the partisan independents."[10]

There are some problems with their classification, however. In particular, it is not clear why voting choices in the presidential election should not be "overtly partisan." Moreover, their scheme would predict less partisanship by leaners on the master-code and most-important-problem items; as tables 5.5 and 5.6 show, leaners' partisan affect on these measures matches or exceeds that of the weak partisans. And as we have seen, respondents' reports about their past voting behavior cannot be relied on.

Nevertheless, the multidimensionality of party identification clearly was an idea whose time had come in the late 1970s.[11] Questions to measure it were among the principal innovations to emerge from the ambitious planning process that preceded the 1980 National Election Study. In addition to the traditional party identification items, respondents were asked:

> In your own mind, do you think of yourself as a supporter of one of the political parties, or not?

10. Ibid., 166.
11. In addition to the articles by Valentine and Van Wingen and by Weisberg, see Richard S. Katz, "The Dimensionality of Party Identification: Cross-National Perspectives," *Comparative Politics* 10 (January 1979): 147–63; Sheldon Kamieniecki, *Party Identification, Political Behavior, and the American Electorate* (Westport, Conn.: Greenwood Press, 1985), and "The Dimensionality of Partisan Strength and Political Independence," *Political Behavior* 10 (Winter 1988): 364–76. Weisberg found ("Multidimensional Conceptualization," 33–34) that party identification "involves separate attitudes toward several distinct objects—political parties generally, the Republican Party, the Democratic Party, and political independence."

Those who answered yes were asked which party they supported and to indicate the strength of that support on a seven-point scale. They were then asked to indicate their closeness to the Republican or Democratic party on a seven-point scale with one party at either end.

People who answered that they were not supporters were asked:

Do you ever think of yourself as closer to one of the two major political parties, or not?

Respondents who said yes were presented with the seven-point scale on which they could designate the degree of their closeness to one or the other party.

Next, *all* respondents were asked:

Do you ever think of yourself as a political Independent, or not?

Those who said yes were asked to indicate "how strongly independent in politics you feel" on a seven-point scale.

Our cross-tabulation of the answers to the questions about being a party supporter and an Independent produced the following four basic types:

1. 24 percent were party supporters, not Independent;
2. 15 percent were party supporters and also Independent;
3. 31 percent were not party supporters and were Independent;
4. 30 percent were neither party supporters nor Independents, a group labeled "the Unattached" by Jack Dennis.[12]

There are some surprises in this new typology. For one thing, just 39 percent appear to have some sort of partisan attach-

12. Jack Dennis, "Political Independence in America, Part I: On Being an Independent Partisan Supporter," *British Journal of Political Science* 18 (January 1988): 85. Few of these items were asked again, by the NES, and almost all were dropped by 1984.

ment, and two-fifths of those claim to be independent as well. More than half the nonsupporters said they were closer to one party; if we add them to the supporters, 66 percent can now be classified as having some kind of partisan affinity. We will return to these "partisan nonsupporters." Can these be all the people in the country with any sort of durable attachment to a party? We mention durability as a criterion because the traditional party identification measure does fairly well in that respect: the distribution of Democrats and Republicans is rather constant, the party system is stable, third parties do not prosper, and all this has been true for many years.

The old party identification measure was under attack because of the apparently anomalous character of the leaners. The articles by Valentine and Van Wingen and by Weisberg led us to expect that the new typology would solve this problem by accommodating leaners in the group of people who called themselves both party supporters and Independents. Indeed, that particular combination, amounting to 15 percent of the sample, seemed tailor-made for leaners, who display both partisan affinities and a preference for thinking of themselves as independent of party. Plausible as this expectation seemed, it was not fulfilled. Only 19 percent of Independent Republicans and 13 percent of Independent Democrats were independent party supporters. A handful of leaners were just plain party supporters. Seventy-five percent of Republican leaners and 85 percent of Democratic leaners were classified as Nonsupporters. This is more than a surprise; it is a serious problem for the new measure because, as we have demonstrated, leaners' voting and attitudes are partisan. These data are set out in table 9.4, which cross-tabulates the old and new measures of partisanship.

Most party nonsupporters conceded, when prodded, that they were closer to one of the two parties. These respondents were asked to locate themselves on "a scale from 1 to 7 where 1 means feeling very close to the Republican party and 7 means feeling very close to the Democratic party." About a fifth chose the midpoint, however, and so cannot be classified as to partisan direction. The others can be combined with the Party Supporters to constitute a group, amounting to 66 percent of the sample, who can be called Democrats or Republicans.

Quite a few categories of strength of partisanship are possible with this schema. Party Supporters, themselves divided into Independents and nonindependents, choose a party and then indicate the strength of their support on a seven-point scale. *In addition*, they locate themselves on the "closeness" scale. Respondents who are not party supporters, likewise divided into Independents and nonindependents, can, on the latter question, indicate any one of three degrees of closeness to a party. The result is a 14-point scale of party support.

This instrument has some problems. As might be expected, many of the categories are underpopulated; three had less than thirty-five cases each in a simple cross-tabulation with political involvement.[13] Putting the points on the scale in the appropriate order required some difficult choices. For example, why is the Democratic pole of the continuum anchored by the "Not Close Independent Democratic Supporters" rather than "Close Independent Democratic Supporters" or "Close Ordinary Democratic Supporters"?[14] What is more, cross-tabulations of this new scale and various measures of belief and behavior produce the same kinds of nonmonotonicity that led to questions about the traditional Michigan party identification questions.[15]

The partisan affinities of leaners were evidently a principal reason—perhaps the only reason—for the surge of interest in exploring other possible dimensions of partisanship. As we have seen, the alternative conceptualization of party identification underlying the 1980 questions shed very little light on people who initially claim to be Independents, concede they are closer to one party, and think and act like partisans. Moreover, introducing independence as a second dimension of

13. Ibid., 96.
14. Ibid., 96–97.
15. Dennis's report on the new partisan supporter measure did not describe its relationship to vote choice.

Table 9.4

Traditional Party Identification and the Party Supporter–Independent Typology, 1980

	Party supporters	Independent party supporters	Independents but not supporters	Neither Independents nor supporters
		Percentage of Each Traditional Category of Party Identification Who Are		
Strong Democrats	58	17	5	19
Weak Democrats	21	12	19	47
Indep. Democrats	2	13	66	19
Pure Independents	1	6	57	36
Indep. Republicans	6	19	60	14
Weak Republicans	26	17	16	41
Strong Republicans	61	23	4	12
All white respondents	24	15	31	30

party identification seems not to improve the traditional measure's power to explain vote choice.

This second dimension may be what Jack Dennis suggests— a manifestation of a need to declare "individuality and autonomy" as political actors, a "self-image of flexibility, adaptability, . . . and willingness to weigh alternatives," an aversion to thinking one makes decisions on the "basis of a fixed and unthinking partisan loyalty."[16] There is no reason why this second dimension could not coexist with a realization of one's partisan affinity. This self-image might be so strong in some partisans as to lead to an initial claim to be an Independent, a claim that is then modified by the subsequent concession of closeness to a party. The two aspects of identity may not be mutually reinforcing, but they do not amount to a contradiction in terms.

While perhaps important to self-esteem, such feelings of autonomy have not been shown to be related to the direction or stability of electoral decisions. What matters is the role of attachment to a party in reaching voting decisions and forming opinions about policies and the performance of the incumbent administration. If some people fit the classic mold of the Independent—above the parties, voting only on the issues and the merits of the candidates—the point is that they are *not partisan*, which is measured on the partisan dimension. If others are not attuned enough to politics to use party labels as cues, the important point is that they are *not partisan*. If one is concerned with swings between the parties, hospitality to third parties, realignment, and so forth, then the important variable is how attached citizens are to one or the other party. This is measured along the partisanship dimension, not the independence dimension.[17]

16. Dennis, "Political Independence, Part I," 87.
17. Morris P. Fiorina makes the point more economically: "This is not to say that 'attitudes toward independence' do not exist nor that they are unimportant, only that it is questionable whether they belong under the concept of party identification"; *Retrospective Voting in American National Elections* (New Haven: Yale University Press, 1981), 105n.

Attitudes toward independence are not the only other dimension that some scholars have discerned. Herbert Weisberg
reports that a "party difference" index formed by subtracting
feeling thermometer ratings for Democrats from ratings for
Republicans did a better job than the party identification
scale of predicting the presidential vote from 1964 through
1976.[18] Sheldon Kamieniecki found the same result for 1980
and concluded that "the party difference index is a superior
measure of partisan direction within the context of electoral
behavior."[19] Both empirical and theoretical considerations
keep us from concluding that these findings are much of an
argument for discarding the traditional party identification
measure. Martin Wattenberg has shown that "although party
identification is a uniquely stable attitudinal variable, evaluations of political parties are not."[20]

Stability, of course, is an essential element of party identification. The familiar question begins, "Generally speaking, do
you usually think of yourself. . . ." Philip Converse explained
that this wording was "originally intended to broaden the time
reference and properly classify the long-term identifier who is
momentarily piqued at his own party, or tempted to defect
temporarily to vote for a charismatic candidate of another
party."[21] The discussions of multidimensionality and attitudes
toward independence and all the rest can distract researchers'
attention from the long-term emotional commitment that en-
dows the concept of party identification with such power. The

18. Weisberg, "A Multidimensional Conceptualization," 44–48.
He reports that the results do not differ substantially if the thermometer stimulus is "Democrats" and "Republicans" or "Democratic party" and "Republican party." For an explicit criticism of
Weisberg, see Michael D. McDonald and Susan E. Howell, "Reconsidering the Reconceptualizations of Party Identification," *Political
Methodology* 8 (1982): 73–91.
19. Kamieniecki, *Party Identification*, 207.
20. Wattenberg, *The Decline of American Political Parties, 1952–
1984*, 31–33. Wattenberg found the same instability in ratings of the
two parties and of "Democrats" and "Republicans."
21. Philip E. Converse, *The Dynamics of Party Support* (Beverly
Hills, Calif.: Sage, 1976), 35.

most famous contemporary party-switcher made this point as well as anyone: "And it's a funny thing about party affiliation, whether you inherit it for generations back in your family. Maybe you embraced it on your own when you were young. But it can be a very wrenching thing, I found, to change parties. You feel as though you're abandoning your past."[22] We doubt that moving 30 degrees on the feeling thermometer would have a similar effect, just as we doubt that anyone ever called himself a "Yellow Dog Independent."

Independent or Apolitical?

In addition to the seven categories of party identification, a few respondents are classified as "apolitical" (see especially table 2.1). Arthur Miller and Martin Wattenberg have drawn attention to the criteria used by the Michigan Center for Political Studies to assign cases to this category when the raw interviews are processed. Individuals who express no preference when answering the sequence of questions about party identification nevertheless are not put in the "apolitical" category unless, judging from their responses to the entire questionnaire (or, before 1966, by looking at an explicit entry on that point by the interviewer), they seemed "virtually totally uninterested and uninformed about politics."[23] Otherwise, they were classified as Pure Independents if they denied being closer to Democrats or Republicans, and as leaners if they acknowledged that they were. The result of this practice is to put in the Independent category some respondents who do not express any preference, even for being an Independent, when first asked about their partisan identity.

Miller and Wattenberg show that there has been an increase in these misclassified respondents since 1968. If they

22. President Ronald Reagan, quoted in *San Francisco Chronicle*, September 20, 1984, A7.
23. Arthur H. Miller and Martin P. Wattenberg, "Measuring Party Identification: Independent or No Partisan Preference?" *American Journal of Political Science* 27 (February 1983): 109.

are tabulated separately from those who claimed to be Independents, it is clear that almost all of the celebrated increase in Independents is due to the no-preference respondents. The proportion of the sample who were acknowledged Independents rose slightly from 1964 to 1968, stayed stable through 1976, and then dropped faintly in 1980. In the latter year, 7.7 percent of the entire sample were acknowledged Pure Independents, compared to 6.7 percent in 1964. The comparable numbers for acknowledged leaners were 16.7 percent for 1980 and 13.9 percent for 1964.

Purifying the Independents by removing the no-preference respondents leads to more impressive showings of civic virtue by both leaners and Pure Independents, with the former still clearly more virtuous. By the same token, the virtue gap between leaners and weak partisans widens, thus intensifying the nonmonotonicity that characterizes the traditional measure.

Other than this lack of monotonicity in relationships between party identification and measures of civic virtue, we see no problems with the traditional measure. In all relationships involving partisan affect, including voting choice, a five-point scale combining leaners and weak partisans seems perfectly satisfactory. We are not uncomfortable with the assertion that the traditional items are an unsatisfactory measure of independence, viewed as a separate dimension from partisanship. This dimension, however, seems important not for explaining voting choice, but, at most, helps understand attitudes toward political parties as such. This is a worthy topic, but it is different from the earth-shaking questions that have been evoked in the large debate about the decline of partisanship.

10

Conclusions

American political parties had always been considered comparatively weak as organizations but strong as sources of identity for the vast majority of citizens.[1] Martin Wattenberg neatly expressed one implication of those identities: "Partisanship once provided the American electorate with a sense of continuity and stability."[2] In the past generation, however, the number of Americans who were "simply and tautologically unconstrained by partisanship"[3] grew to a point where they were assessed as "the largest group in the society."[4] The peo-

1. The still fairly limited comparative research suggests that party identification is more widespread, stable, and important in the United States than in other democracies. See Ian Budge, Ivor Crewe, and Dennis Farlie, eds., *Party Identification and Beyond* (New York: John Wiley and Sons, 1976); Richard G. Niemi and Herbert F. Weisberg, "Is Party Identification Meaningful?" in *Controversies in Voting Behavior*, 2d ed., ed. Niemi and Weisberg (Washington, D.C.: CQ Press, 1984).

2. Martin P. Wattenberg, *The Decline of American Political Parties, 1952–1984* (Cambridge: Harvard University Press, 1986), 130.

3. Gerald M. Pomper, *Voter's Choice* (New York: Harper and Row, 1975), 40.

4. Norman H. Nie, Sidney Verba, and John R. Petrocik, *The Changing American Voter*, enlarged ed. (Cambridge: Harvard University Press, 1979), 346.

ple in this group were "adrift without an anchor in a political world full of strong eddies and currents."[5]

The significance of the growing number of Independents was thought by many observers to be far more profound than merely increasing the number of people who no longer voted reflexively for a party, irrespective of any other consideration. "The independent vote is up for grabs."[6] Political parties were weakened, and the consequences were likely to be unwelcome:

> This growing dissolution of party-in-the-electorate entails a serious erosion of political parties as basic institutional components of the political system. . . . The progressive disappearance of party . . . would appear to favor political instability and ineffective performance on a scale without recent precedent.[7]

All the anxiety—or eager anticipation, as the case may be—about the impending volatility of the American political system was misplaced. It assumed that people without party ties really did amount to nearly two-fifths of the electorate. In fact, at their peak, genuine neutrals were a mere 15 percent of the population and never amounted to more than 11 percent of those who cast their ballots in a national election. Most of the people who initially told an interviewer that they were Independents conceded when asked that they were closer to one or the other major party. Those who leaned toward the Democratic party were very similar to outright Democrats in their voting habits, opinions on the issues, and views of the

5. Wattenberg, *The Decline of American Political Parties*, 130.

6. William Crotty, *American Parties in Decline*, 2d ed. (Boston: Little, Brown, 1984), 37.

7. Walter Dean Burnham, *The Current Crisis in American Politics* (New York: Oxford University Press, 1982), 207, 244. Surveying the literature on changes in party identification, the late Philip Williams observed that Burnham "hinted repeatedly at very drastic implications, foreshadowing a *crise de régime* with unpredictable but probably apocalyptic consequences." "Review Article: Party Realignment in the United States and Britain," *British Journal of Political Science* 15 (January 1985): 103.

Democratic party. The same was true of people who initially labeled themselves Independents and then admitted they were closer to the Republican party. People who denied they were closer to either party were, on all these measures, in between Democrats and Republicans. They were also less likely to vote, to have opinions, or to care about politics. Broadly defined Independents, which is the way most scholars and journalists defined them, had nothing in common except a disinclination to think of themselves as partisans.

The increase in all three kinds of Independents began in the mid-1960s, reached its peak a decade later, and is slowly ebbing. It was greatest among people who reached voting age in this period, somewhat evident in the next-oldest generation, and all but invisible among people who were in their 40s by the beginning of the period. All the evidence is not in on the long-term durability of this trend; current data suggest it is fading. The generation in question is becoming more partisan but still contains fewer outright partisans than its counterpart generation twenty years earlier. People now entering the electorate are less partisan than their counterparts from the early 1960s but more partisan than those from the late 1960s and early 1970s.

A "shock" to partisanship indisputably occurred a generation ago.[8] The source of that shock is something of a puzzle, however. It did not seem to be a result of public dissatisfaction with the conduct of the Vietnam War or the simultaneous problem of urban unrest. Nor could it be located in ideologues' rejection of the doctrinal adequacy of either party.[9] Pure Independents were a bit more common among people who seemed alienated from the American political system,

8. The term was used in this context by Philip E. Converse, who discerned one shock in the mid-1960s and another in 1971–1974. See his *The Dynamics of Party Support* (Beverly Hills, Calif.: Sage, 1976).

9. The notion that a higher level of political consciousness freed some Americans of a need to rely on parties as cognitive devices has been thoroughly refuted by Eric R.A.N. Smith, *The Unchanging American Voter* (Berkeley: University of California Press, 1990).

and also among those who expressed disapproval of political parties as institutions. The latter attitude may have accounted for some of the leaners' unwillingness to acknowledge identification with a party. For the most part, the leaners are still something of a mystery. The attempt in 1980 to explain how people could be both partisan and independent was largely unsuccessful.

Explaining leaners loses much of its importance, however, if one recognizes that what is to be explained is not a pattern of belief, behavior, or commitment. What is to be explained is a questionnaire response. While not intending to deprecate this as a research topic, we think it important to say that shedding light on leaners has more to do with exploring self-images than threats to domestic stability.

Do Parties Matter Any More?

Throughout this book we have assumed that parties matter, that it is worthwhile to be concerned about the numbers and characteristics of the various kinds of Democrats, Republicans, and Independents. Arguing that the growth of Independents has been widely misconstrued because leaners resemble partisans, we have attempted to refute one verse in the "decline of the parties" litany that is familiar to every attentive undergraduate and every public-spirited adult. But there is another verse in the litany: parties are unimportant among the public because they have nothing much to do with how people vote or think about the world. Here are examples of this line of thought:

> Party identification is chiefly interesting as a predictor of how people will vote ... and how they can be expected to continue to vote in the future. But both the election results reported earlier and the volatility and inconclusiveness of trends in party sentiment emphasized here give reason to doubt the usefulness of identification data in making such predictions. ... American

voters . . . seem to resort less and less to parties as a key to their vote at all.[10]

There is an increasing willingness on the part of many party members to break with their party and its candidates and to vote for the opposition.[11]

Chapter 4 provided a good deal of evidence that generalizations like these were wide of the mark (see especially tables 4.1 and 4.2). Here we make the same point with data about the relationship of party identification to vote choice in elections from the 1950s to 1990. Table 10.1 classifies all voters, including blacks, into one of these three categories: people (including leaners) who identified with a party and voted for that party's candidate; party identifiers who voted for another party's candidate; and Pure Independents. These data are presented separately for presidential and House elections.

The trend line for Pure Independents in presidential contests is essentially flat, varying within a range of four percentage points in the nine elections from 1956 through 1988. The two elections with the smallest proportion of Pure Independents were in 1964 and 1988. The trend for defectors displays greater variation but no consistent pattern. In six of the nine elections, the proportion of defectors varied from a low of 12 percent in 1988 to a high of 17 percent in 1976. The differences verge on the trivial, as they do for Pure Independents. In 1968 and 1980, when there were major third-party candidates, George Wallace and John Anderson, the proportion of defectors rose to 23 and 24 percent; every partisan who voted for either man was a defector. The high point of defection was reached in 1972 and largely reflects George McGovern's singular lack of appeal to most Democrats.

The data for House elections show a trend toward more

10. Thomas Ferguson and Joel Rogers, *Right Turn: The Decline of the Democrats and the Future of American Politics* (New York: Hill and Wang, 1986), 32.
11. Crotty, *American Parties in Decline*, 31.

Table 10.1
Composition of Voters in Presidential and House Elections, 1956–1990

	Presidential Elections			House Elections		
	Party-line voters[a]	Defectors[b]	Pure Indeps.	Party-line voters[a]	Defectors[b]	Pure Indeps.
1956	76	15	9	82	9	9
1958				84	11	5
1960	79	13	8	80	11	9
1962				83	11	6
1964	79	16	6	80	16	5
1966				76	17	7
1968	69	23	9	74	19	7
1970				76	16	9
1972	67	25	9	75	17	8
1974				74	18	8
1976	73	17	10	72	19	9
1978				67	23	10
1980	68	24	9	69	23	8
1982				76	17	6
1984	79	13	8	70	23	7
1986				72	22	6
1988	81	12	7	74	20	7
1990				75	20	5

Note: The entry in each cell is the proportion of all voters, except apoliticals, in the indicated election who voted for their own party's candidate, for another party's candidate, or were Pure Independents.
[a]Strong, weak, and independent partisans who voted for their party's candidate for president or for the House of Representatives.
[b]Strong, weak, and independent partisans who voted for another party's candidate. All partisans who voted for George Wallace or John Anderson were defectors.

defectors, who averaged 10 percent of all voters in the 1950s, 15 percent in the 1960s, 18 percent in the 1970s, and 21 percent in the most recent decade. Here is evidence that party loyalty is declining in House elections, but even so the extent of party-line voting is far greater than the quoted passages would lead one to believe.

The other relevant data are Warren Miller's correlations of party identification with presidential vote choice in every election from 1952 through 1988. In a bivariate correlation in which party identification was the only independent variable, the two highest coefficients were in the two most recent elections, the two lowest in 1964 and 1972, and no consistent trend could be discerned. Miller then introduced controls for race, education, gender, religion, income, and union membership. Partial correlation coefficients above .60 were found in 1952 and 1956, and again from 1976 through 1988. The lowest coefficient (.43) was found for 1972.[12] These data reinforce those in table 10.1 to make the same point: There has been no decline in the power of party identification to predict vote choices in presidential elections. Americans in the 1980s voted along party lines as frequently as in the 1950s.

We conclude on a doubly cheerful note. As political scientists, we are reassured to learn that party identification should remain a central concept in the study of individual political behavior and that the traditional method of measuring it has not been seriously threatened. As citizens, we take heart from our findings that the surface-level increase in Independents does not portend a decline in political stability, the decay of the political system, nor any of the other unwelcome developments heralded by some scholars. In fact, we might go so far as to say that it portends very little at all.

12. Warren E. Miller, "Party Identification, Realignment, and Party Voting: Back to the Basics," *American Political Science Review* 85 (June 1991): 565. In these computations only weak and strong partisans were considered to have any inclination toward a party; leaners were included with Pure Independents.

Appendix

Items in the National Election Studies
Alienation Indexes

Institutional Responsiveness Index

1. Over the years, how much attention do you feel the government pays to what the people think when it decides what to do: a good deal, some, or not much?
2. How much do you feel that political parties help to make the government pay attention to what the people think: a good deal, some, or not much?
3. And how much do you feel that having elections makes the government pay attention to what the people think: a good deal, some, or not much?
4. How much attention do you think most congressmen pay to the people who elect them when they decide what to do in Congress: a good deal, some, or not much?

Trust-in-Government Index

1. Do you think that people in the government waste a lot of money we pay in taxes, waste some of it, or don't waste very much of it?
2. How much of the time do you think you can trust the government in Washington to do what is right—just about always, most of the time, or only some of the time?
3. Would you say the government is pretty much run by a few big interests looking out for themselves or that it is run for the benefit of all the people?

4. Do you feel that almost all of the people running the government are smart people who usually know what they are doing, or do you think that quite a few of them don't seem to know what they are doing?
5. Do you think that quite a few of the people running the government are a little crooked, not very many are, or do you think hardly any of them are crooked at all?

Political Efficacy Index

(All items are agree-disagree.)
1. People like me don't have any say about what the government does.
2. Voting is the only way that people like me can have any say about how the government runs things.
3. Sometimes politics and government seem so complicated that a person like me can't really understand what's going on.
4. I don't think public officials care much what people like me think.

Bibliography

Abramson, Paul R. "Developing Party Identification: A Further Examination of Life-Cycle, Generational, and Period Effects." *American Journal of Political Science* 23 (February 1979): 78–96.

———. "Generational Change and the Decline of Party Identification in America, 1952–1974." *American Political Science Review* 70 (June 1976): 469–78.

———. "Generational Replacement and Partisan Dealignment in Britain and the United States." *British Journal of Political Science* 8 (July 1978): 505–9.

Abramson, Paul R., John H. Aldrich, and David W. Rohde. *Change and Continuity in the 1980 Elections*. Rev. ed. Washington: CQ Press, 1983.

Abramson, Paul R., and Charles W. Ostrom, Jr. "Macropartisanship: An Empirical Reassessment." *American Political Science Review* 85 (March 1991): 138–47.

Asher, Herbert B. *Presidential Elections and American Politics: Voters, Candidates and Campaigns since 1952*. 4th ed. Chicago: Dorsey Press, 1988.

Beck, Paul Allen. "Incomplete Realignment: The Reagan Legacy for Parties and Elections." In *The Reagan Legacy: Promise and Performance*, edited by Charles O. Jones, 145–71. Chatham, N.J.: Chatham House, 1988.

Boyd, Richard W. "Popular Control of Public Policy: A Normal Vote Analysis of the 1968 Election." *American Political Science Review* 66 (June 1972): 429–49.

Brody, Richard A. "Stability and Change in Party Identification: Presidential to Off-Years." In *Reasoning and Choice: Explorations in Political Psychology,* edited by Paul M. Sniderman, Richard A. Brody, and Philip E. Tetlock. New York: Cambridge University Press, 1991.

Budge, Ian, Ivor Crewe, and Dennis Farlie, eds. *Party Identification and Beyond.* New York: John Wiley and Sons, 1976.

Burnham, Walter Dean. *Critical Elections and the Mainsprings of American Politics.* New York: W. W. Norton, 1970.

————. "The End of American Party Politics." *Transaction* 7 (December 1969): 12–22.

Campbell, Angus, Philip E. Converse, Warren E. Miller, and Donald E. Stokes. *The American Voter.* New York: John Wiley and Sons, 1960.

————. *Elections and the Political Order.* New York: John Wiley and Sons, 1966.

Campbell, Angus, Gerald Gurin, and Warren E. Miller. *The Voter Decides.* Evanston, Ill.: Row, Peterson, 1954.

Citrin, Jack. "Comment: The Political Relevance of Trust in Government." *American Political Science Review* 68 (September 1974): 973–88.

Converse, Philip E. *The Dynamics of Party Support: Analyzing Party Identification.* Beverly Hills, Calif.: Sage, 1976.

————. "The Nature of Belief Systems in Mass Publics." In *Ideology and Discontent,* edited by David Apter, 206–61. New York: Free Press, 1964.

Converse, Philip E., and Gregory B. Markus. "Plus ça change . . . : The New CPS Election Study Panel." *American Political Science Review* 73 (March 1979): 32–49.

Converse, Philip E., and Roy Pierce. "Measuring Partisanship." *Political Methodology* 11 (1985): 143–66.

Craig, Steven C. "Partisanship, Independence, and No Preference: Another Look at the Measurement of Party Identification." *American Journal of Political Science* 29 (May 1985): 274–90.

Crotty, William J. *American Parties in Decline.* 2d ed. Boston: Little, Brown, 1984.

Dennis, Jack. "New Measures of Partisanship in Models of Voting." Paper delivered at the 1982 annual meeting of the Midwest Political Science Association.

———. "Political Independence in America, Part I: On Being an Independent Partisan Supporter." *British Journal of Political Science* 18 (January 1988): 77–109.

———. "Public Support for the Party System, 1964–1984." Paper delivered at the 1986 annual meeting of the American Political Science Association.

———. "Some Properties of Measures of Partisanship." Paper delivered at the 1981 annual meeting of the American Political Science Association.

———. "Support for the Party System by the Mass Public." *American Political Science Review* 60 (September 1966): 600–615.

———. "Political Independence in America, Part II: Towards a Theory." *British Journal of Political Science* 18 (April 1988): 197–219.

Epstein, Leon D. *Political Parties in the American Mold.* Madison: University of Wisconsin Press, 1986.

Finkel, Steven E., and Howard A. Scarrow. "Party Identification and Party Enrollment: The Difference and the Consequence." *Journal of Politics* 47 (May 1985): 620–42.

Fiorina, Morris P. *Retrospective Voting in American National Elections.* New Haven: Yale University Press, 1981.

Flanigan, William H., and Nancy H. Zingale. *Political Behavior of the American Electorate.* 6th ed. Boston: Allyn and Bacon, 1987.

Franklin, Charles H. "Issue Preferences, Socialization, and the Evolution of Party Identification." *American Journal of Political Science* 28 (August 1984): 459–78.

Franklin, Charles H., and John E. Jackson. "The Dynamics of Party Identification." *American Political Science Review* 77 (December 1983): 957–73.

Gant, Michael M., and Norman R. Luttbeg. "The Cognitive Utility of Partisanship." *Western Political Quarterly* 40 (September 1987): 499–517.

Gilmour, Robert, and Robert Lamb. *Political Alienation in Contemporary America*. New York: St. Martin's Press, 1975.

Green, Donald Philip, and Bradley Palmquist. "Of Artifacts and Partisan Instability." *American Journal of Political Science* 34 (August 1990): 872–902.

Jacoby, William G. "The Impact of Party Identification on Issue Attitudes." *American Journal of Political Science* 32 (August 1988): 643–61.

Jennings, M. Kent, and Gregory B. Markus. "Partisan Orientations over the Long Haul: Results from the Three-Wave Political Socialization Panel Study." *American Political Science Review* 78 (December 1984): 1000–1018.

Jennings, M. Kent, and Richard G. Niemi. "The Persistence of Political Orientations: An Over-Time Analysis of Two Generations." *British Journal of Political Science* 8 (July 1978): 333–63.

Kamieniecki, Sheldon. "The Dimensionality of Partisan Strength and Political Independence." *Political Behavior* 10 (Winter 1988): 364–76.

Katz, Richard S. "The Dimensionality of Party Identification: Cross-National Perspectives." *Comparative Politics* 10 (January 1979): 147–63.

Keith, Bruce E., David B. Magleby, Candice J. Nelson, Elizabeth Orr, Mark C. Westlye, and Raymond E. Wolfinger. "The Myth of the Independent Voter." Paper delivered at the 1977 annual meeting of the American Political Science Association.

———. "The Partisan Affinities of Independent 'Leaners.'" *British Journal of Political Science* 16 (April 1986): 155–85.

Kessel, John H. *Presidential Campaign Politics*. 2d ed. Homewood, Ill.: Dorsey Press, 1984.

Key, V. O., Jr., and Frank Munger. "Social Determinism and Electoral Decision: The Case of Indiana." In *American Voting Behavior*, edited by Eugene Burdick and Arthur J. Brodbeck. New York: Free Press, 1959.

Kinder, Donald R., and David O. Sears. "Public Opinion and Political Action." In *Handbook of Social Psychology*, vol. 2,

3d ed., edited by Gardner Lindzey and Elliot Aronson, 659–741. New York: Random House, 1985.

Konda, Thomas M., and Lee Sigelman. "Public Evaluations of the American Parties, 1952–1984." *The Journal of Politics* 49 (August 1987): 814–29.

Ladd, Everett Carll, Jr. "As the Realignment Turns: A Drama in Many Acts." *Public Opinion* 7 (December–January 1985): 2–7.

———. "The Brittle Mandate: Electoral Dealignment and the 1980 Presidential Election." *Political Science Quarterly* 96 (Spring 1981): 1–25.

———. "Declarations of Independents." *Public Opinion* 7 (April–May 1984): 21–32.

———. "The Shifting Party Coalitions—from the 1930s to the 1970s." In *Party Coalitions in the 1980s*, edited by Seymour Martin Lipset, 127–49. San Francisco: Institute for Contemporary Studies, 1981.

———. *Where Have All the Voters Gone?* 2d ed. New York: W. W. Norton, 1982.

Ladd, Everett Carll, Jr., Charles D. Hadley, and Lauriston King. "A New Political Alignment." In *Political Opinion and Behavior: Essays and Studies*, 3d ed., edited by Edward C. Dreyer and Walter A. Rosenbaum, 136–50. North Scituate, Mass.: Duxbury Press, 1976.

Luskin, Robert C., John P. McIver, and Edward G. Carmines. "Issues and the Transmission of Partisanship." *American Journal of Political Science* 33 (May 1989): 440–58.

McDonald, Michael D., and Susan E. Howell. "Reconsidering the Reconceptualizations of Party Identification." *Political Methodology* 8 (1982): 73–91.

MacKuen, Michael B., Robert S. Erikson, and James A. Stimson. "Macropartisanship." *American Political Science Review* 83 (December 1989): 1125–42.

Mann, Thomas E., and Raymond E. Wolfinger. "Candidates and Parties in Congressional Elections." *American Political Science Review* 74 (September 1980): 617–32.

Markus, Gregory B. "Dynamic Modeling of Cohort Change:

The Case of Political Partisanship." *American Journal of Political Science* 27 (November 1983): 717–39.

Miller, Arthur H. "Political Issues and Trust in Government." *American Political Science Review* 68 (September 1974): 951–72.

Miller, Arthur H., and Warren E. Miller. "Partisanship and Performance: 'Rational' Choice in the 1976 Presidential Election." Paper delivered at the 1977 annual meeting of the American Political Science Association.

Miller, Arthur H., and Martin P. Wattenberg. "Measuring Party Identification: Independent or No Partisan Preference?" *American Journal of Political Science* 27 (February 1983): 106–21.

Miller, Warren E. "Party Identification, Realignment, and Party Voting: Back to the Basics." *American Political Science Review* 85 (June 1991): 557–68.

———. "The Cross-National Use of Party Identification as a Stimulus to Political Inquiry." In *Party Identification and Beyond: Representations of Voting and Party Competition*, edited by Ian Budge, Ivor Crewe, and Dennis Farlie, 21–31. New York: John Wiley and Sons, 1976.

———. "Party Identification Re-examined: The Reagan Era." In Miller and John R. Petrocik, *Where's the Party? An Assessment of Changes in Party Loyalty and Party Coalitions in the 1980s*, 9–29. Washington, D.C.: Center for National Policy, 1987.

Miller, Warren E., and Teresa E. Levitin. *Leadership and Change: Presidential Elections from 1952 to 1976*. Cambridge, Mass.: Winthrop, 1976.

Muller, Edward N., and Thomas O. Jukam. "On the Meaning of Political Support." *American Political Science Review* 71 (December 1977): 1561–95.

Nie, Norman H., Sidney Verba, and John R. Petrocik. *The Changing American Voter*. Enlarged ed. Cambridge: Harvard University Press, 1979.

Niemi, Richard G., Richard S. Katz, and David Newman. "Reconstructing Past Partisanship: The Failure of the Party

Identification Recall Questions." *American Journal of Political Science* 24 (November 1980): 633–51.

Niemi, Richard G., Stephen Wright, and Lynda W. Powell. "Multiple Party Identifiers and the Measurement of Party Identification." *Journal of Politics* 49 (November 1987): 1093–1103.

Norpoth, Helmut. "Under Way and Here to Stay: Party Realignment in the 1980s?" *Public Opinion Quarterly* 51 (Fall 1987): 376–91.

Norpoth, Helmut, and Jerrold C. Rusk. "Partisan Dealignment in the American Electorate: Itemizing the Deductions since 1964." *American Political Science Review* 76 (September 1982): 522–37.

Page, Benjamin I., and Richard A. Brody. "Policy Voting and the Electoral Process: The Vietnam War Issue." *American Political Science Review* 66 (September 1972): 979–95.

Page, Benjamin I., and Raymond E. Wolfinger. "Party Identification." In *Readings in American Political Behavior*, 2d ed., edited by Raymond E. Wolfinger. Englewood Cliffs, N.J.: Prentice-Hall, 1970.

Petrocik, John R. "An Analysis of Intransitivities in the Index of Party Identification." *Political Methodology* 1 (Summer 1974): 31–47.

———. "Contextual Sources of Voting Behavior: The Changeable American Voter." In *The Electorate Reconsidered*, edited by John C. Pierce and John L. Sullivan, 257–77. Beverly Hills, Calif.: Sage, 1980.

———. "An Expected Party Vote: New Data for an Old Concept." *American Journal of Political Science* 33 (February 1989): 44–66.

———. *Party Coalitions*. Chicago: University of Chicago Press, 1981.

Pierce, John C., and Paul R. Hagner. "Conceptualization and Party Identification: 1956–76."*American Journal of Political Science* 26 (May 1982): 377–87.

Pomper, Gerald M. *Voter's Choice*. New York: Harper and Row, 1975.

Pomper, Gerald M., and Susan S. Lederman. *Elections in America.* 2d ed. New York: Longman, 1980.

Pomper, Gerald M., Ross K. Baker, Charles E. Jacob, Wilson Carey McWilliams, Henry A. Plotkin, (with) Marlene M. Pomper, eds. *The Election of 1976.* New York: David McKay, 1977.

Ranney, Austin. *Curing the Mischiefs of Faction: Party Reform in America.* Berkeley: University of California Press, 1975.

Schneider, William. "Antipartisanship in America." In *Parties and Democracy in Britain and America,* edited by Vernon Bogdanor, 103–44. New York: Praeger, 1984.

———. "The November 6 Vote for President: What Did It Mean?" In *The American Election of 1984,* edited by Austin Ranney, 99–126. Durham, N.C.: Duke University Press, 1985.

Schreiber, E. M. " 'Where the Ducks Are': Southern Strategy versus Fourth Party." *Public Opinion Quarterly* 35 (Summer 1971): 157–67.

Shively, W. Phillips. "The Development of Party Identification Among Adults: Exploration of a Functional Model." *American Political Science Review* 73 (December 1979): 1039–54.

———. "The Nature of Party Identification: A Review of Recent Developments." In *The Electorate Reconsidered,* edited by John C. Pierce and John L. Sullivan, 219–36. Beverly Hills, Calif.: Sage, 1980.

Sigelman, Lee, Philip W. Roeder, Malcolm E. Jewell, and Michael A. Baer. "Voting and Nonvoting: A Multi-Election Perspective." *American Journal of Political Science* 29 (November 1985): 749–65.

Stanley, Harold W. "Southern Partisan Changes: Dealignment, Realignment or Both?" *Journal of Politics* 50 (February 1988): 64–88.

Valentine, David, and John Van Wingen. "Partisanship, Independence, and the Partisan Identification Question." *American Politics Quarterly* 8 (April 1980): 165–86.

Wattenberg, Martin P. *The Decline of American Political Parties, 1952–1984.* Cambridge: Harvard University Press, 1986.

————. "The Decline of Political Partisanship in the United States: Negativity or Neutrality?" *American Political Science Review* 75 (December 1981): 941–50.

————. "The Hollow Realignment: Partisan Change in a Candidate-Centered Era." *Public Opinion Quarterly* 51 (Spring 1987): 58–74.

Weisberg, Herbert F. "A Multidimensional Conceptualization of Party Identification." *Political Behavior* 2 (1980): 33–60.

Wolfinger, Raymond E., and Michael G. Hagen. "Republican Prospects: Southern Comfort." *Public Opinion* 8 (October–November 1985): 8–13.

Wolfinger, Raymond E., and Steven J. Rosenstone. *Who Votes?* New Haven: Yale University Press, 1980.

Index

222   *Index*

Compositor: Huron Valley Graphics
Text: 10/13 Aster
Display: Helvetica Condensed
Printer: Maple-Vail Book Mfg. Group
Binder: Maple-Vail Book Mfg. Group